STATE OF TH

W.B. Ye

State of the Art series

Geoffrey Chaucer, Anne Rooney
Christopher Marlowe, William Tydeman & Vivien Thomas
W.B. Yeats, David Pierce

Forthcoming
George Eliot, Graham Handley
Nathaniel Hawthorne, Allan Lloyd Smith
Virginia Woolf, John Mepham
Thomas Hardy, Charles Lock
D.H. Lawrence, Damian Grant
Henry Vaughan and George Herbert, Alan Rudrum
Percy Bysshe Shelley, Michael Rossington
William Blake, Steven Vine
Joseph Conrad, Robert Hampson & Owen Knowles

STATE OF THE ART

W.B. YEATS

A guide through the critical maze

David Pierce

THE BRISTOL PRESS

For Mary and Matthew, labourers also

The Bristol Press is an imprint of
Bristol Classical Press, 226 North Street, Bedminster, Bristol BS3 1JD

British Library Cataloguing in Publication Data
Pierce, David
W.B. Yeats. – (State of the art series)
1. Poetry in English. Yeats, W.B. (William Butler),
1865-1939
I. Title II. Series
821'.8

ISBN 1-85399-076-0
ISBN 1-85399-077-9 pbk

Printed and bound in Great Britain by
Billing & Sons Ltd, Worcester

Contents

Acknowledgements vii

Note on the Text vii

List of Abbreviations viii

List of Yeats' Other Works x

Chapter 1: Introduction 1
- Preliminary Remarks 1
- Biographies of Yeats 2
- Introductory Studies 5
- Bibliographical Details 8

Chapter 2: Yeats' Poetry 13
- The Process of Composition 13
- The Order of the Poems 20
  - *'The Sacred Book of the Arts'* 20
  - *The Finneran debate* 22
- The Reception of Yeats' Verse 26
  - *An early trilogy* 26
  - *Yeats and symbolism* 29
  - *Yeats' lineage* 33
  - *Yeats' poetry and his beliefs* 40

Chapter 3: Yeats' Drama 48
- Introductions and Texts 48
- Yeats' Theatre 51
  - *The poet in the theatre* 51
  - *The Abbey Theatre* 52
  - *'An unpopular theatre'* 58
- Yeats' Plays 61
  - *The Cuchulain cycle* 61
  - *Last plays* 63

Chapter 4: Yeats' Prose 69
Yeats as Story-teller 69
Yeats and Autobiography 72
A Vision and the Occult 79
Yeats' occult activities 79
Per Amica Silentia Lunae 82
A Vision 83

Chapter 5: Yeats and the Irish Context 96
Yeats and 19th-Century Ireland 96
Yeats and the oral tradition 96
Yeats and the literary tradition 99
Yeats and 18th-Century Ireland 101
Yeats and Modern Ireland 103
Yeats in his own period 103
Yeats and later Irish writers 107
Yeats and Fascism 109

Chapter 6: Yeats and the Contemporary Critical Perspective 116
Yeats and Literary Language 116
Yeats and Women 118
Yeats and the Visual Arts 121
Yeats and Modern Literature 124
Yeats and Nietzsche 124
Yeats and modernism 127
Yeats and modern culture 131

Bibliography 136

Acknowledgements

I would like to register here my gratitude to the Librarian of the College of Ripon and York St John and her staff – especially Sandra Huxley – for their work on my behalf. I am also indebted to Graham Martin and to Timothy Webb for taking an interest in my work on Yeats, and to Terry Eagleton, W.J. McCormack and George J. Watson for much helpful advice. Timothy Webb kindly read and commented on what I thought was a final draft to this book. Michael Bird, my editor at Bristol Classical Press, should also be thanked at this stage for the careful and tactful way he handled the progress from draft to book. My chief debt is to my wife Mary Eagleton, who more than anyone helped me see what I wanted to say.

Note on the Text

To ensure the text remains relatively uncluttered, abbreviations for Yeats' most frequently cited works have been used and titles kept to a minimum. Thus, instead of William Butler Yeats, *The Wild Swans at Coole* (Cuala Press, 1917) or Frank Kermode, *Romantic Image* (1957; repr. Collins, 1976), I have substituted simply *WSC* and Kermode (1957). The list of abbreviations, together with information about other Yeats titles, appears at the beginning of the book, the Bibliography at the end. Less frequently cited works by Yeats are keyed to the 'List of Yeats' Other Works'. Thus Yeats, 1940 stands for William Butler Yeats, *Letters on Poetry from W.B. Yeats to Dorothy Wellesley* (1940; repr. introd. Kathleen Raine, Oxford University Press, 1964).

List of Abbreviations

(This follows for the most part the list of abbreviations to be found in Jeffares' *A New Commentary On the Poems of W.B. Yeats*, 1984).

A	*Autobiographies* (Macmillan, 1955)
ATHW	*At the Hawk's Well* (1916); repr. in *Four Plays for Dancers* (Macmillan, 1921)
AV	*A Vision*
AVA	*A Vision* (1925); repr. *A Critical Edition of Yeats' A Vision* (1925), eds George Mills Harper and Walter Kelly Hood (Macmillan, 1978)
AVB	*A Vision* (1937; repr. Macmillan, 1962)
CK	*The Countess Kathleen and Various Legends and Lyrics* (T. Fisher Unwin, 1892) (In subsequent printings and versions the title was changed to *The Countess Cathleen*)
CL	*The Collected Letters of W.B. Yeats*, volume one 1865-95, eds John Kelly and Eric Domville (Clarendon Press, 1985)
CP	*Collected Poems* (Macmillan, 1950)
CPl	*The Collected Plays of W.B. Yeats* (Macmillan, 1952)
CT	*The Celtic Twilight* (Lawrence and Bullen, 1893)
DC	*The Death of Cuchulain* (1939); repr. in *Last Poems and Two Plays* (Cuala Press, 1939)
Ex	*Explorations* sel. Mrs W.B. Yeats (UK: Macmillan, 1962; USA: Macmillan, 1963)
E & I	*Essays and Introductions* (Macmillan, 1961)
GH	*The Green Helmet and Other Poems* (Cuala Press, 1910)
L	*The Letters of W.B. Yeats*, ed. Allan Wade (Rupert Hart-Davis, 1954)
LP	*Last Poems* (as in *CP*)
LP (PNE)	*Last Poems* (as in *PNE*)
M	*Mythologies* (Macmillan, 1959)
NP	*New Poems* (Cuala Press, 1938)

P	*Purgatory* (1939); repr. in *Last Poems and Two Plays* (Cuala Press, 1939)
PASL	*Per Amica Silentia Lunae* (Macmillan, 1918)
PNE	*W.B. Yeats: The Poems A New Edition*, ed. Richard J. Finneran (Macmillan, 1984)
PY	*The Poems of W.B. Yeats*, 2 vols (Macmillan, 1949)
R	*Reveries over Childhood and Youth* (Macmillan, 1916)
SB	*The Speckled Bird*, with Variant Versions, ed. William H. O'Donnell (McClelland and Stewart, 1976)
SR	*The Secret Rose* (Lawrence and Bullen, 1897)
SW	*The Shadowy Waters* (Hodder and Stoughton, 1900)
T	*The Tower* (Macmillan, 1928)
VE	*The Variorum Edition of the Poems of W.B. Yeats*, eds Peter Allt and Russell K. Alspach (1957; repr. Macmillan, 1966)
VPl	*The Variorum Edition of the Plays of W.B. Yeats*, ed. Russell K. Alspach (1966; repr. Macmillan, 1979)
WO	*The Wanderings of Oisin and Other Poems* (Kegan Paul Trench and Co., 1889)
WR	*The Wind Among the Reeds* (Elkin Mathews, 1899)
WS	*The Winding Stair and Other Poems* (Macmillan, 1933)
WSC	*The Wild Swans at Coole* (Cuala Press, 1917)

List of Yeats' Other Works

Fairy and Folk Tales of the Irish Peasantry (Walter Scott, 1888)
Stories from Carleton (Walter Scott, 1889)
The Collected Works of W.B. Yeats 8 vols (A.H. Bullen, 1908)
Plays for an Irish Theatre, with designs by Gordon Craig (A.H. Bullen, 1911)
Letters on Poetry from W.B. Yeats to Dorothy Wellesley (1940; repr. introd. Kathleen Raine, Oxford University Press, 1964)
W.B. Yeats and T. Surge Moore: Their Correspondence 1901-1937, ed. Ursula Bridges (1953; repr. Greenwood Press, 1978)
'Modern Ireland: an Address to American Audiences 1932-1933', ed. Curtis Bradford, *Massachusetts Review* v (1964), pp. 256-68
Samhain October 1901-November 1908, repr. introd. B.C. Bloomfield (Frank Cass, 1970)
Beltaine, May 1899-April 1900, repr. introd. B.C. Bloomfield (Frank Cass, 1970a)
Uncollected Prose by W.B. Yeats 1, ed. John Frayne (Macmillan, 1970)
Uncollected Prose by W.B. Yeats 2, eds John Frayne and Colton Johnson (Macmillan, 1975)
The Secret Rose: Stories by W.B. Yeats: A Variorum Edition, eds Phillip Marcus, Warwick Gould and Michael Sidnell (Cornell University Press, 1981)
The Death of Cuchulain: Manuscript Materials Including the Author's Final Text, ed. Phillip Marcus (Cornell University Press, 1982)
Purgatory: Manuscript Materials Including the Author's Final Text, ed. Sandra Siegel (Cornell University Press, 1984)
The Early Poetry: Vol 1: 'Mosada' and 'The Island of Statues': Manuscript Materials Including the Author's Final Text, ed. George Bornstein (Cornell University Press, 1987)
(Written with Lady Gregory), *Where There is Nothing and The Unicorn From the Stars*, ed. Katherine Worth (USA: Catholic University of America; UK: Colin Smythe, 1988)

Chapter 1
Introduction

Preliminary Remarks

This guide to Yeats criticism presumes a certain familiarity with the primary Yeats texts. The best criticism challenges our assumptions of reading and draws our attention to unnoticed aspects of a text, but it always remains an ancillary occupation, forever dependent on the quiet savouring of the original text. The history and sociology of Yeats criticism has important uses and can extend our knowledge of the writer, but it can never replace the active, imaginative involvement on the part of the reader. This account of Yeats criticism accepts, therefore, the limitations of such an inquiry, while at the same time recognising two provisos: firstly, that all criticism attempts to come between the reader and the text, and, secondly, that all texts read us as much as we read them.

The ideal way to read Yeats is from start to finish, from *The Wanderings of Oisin* (*WO*, 1889) to *The Death of Cuchulain* (*DC*, 1939), but for the student encountering Yeats on a modern literature course this is a daunting, if not impossible, task. After studying Yeats, students often feel perplexed – a mixture of fascination for his strange ideas, an appreciation of his early love poems, astonishment at the compression of thought in a poem such as 'Among School Children', but an uneasiness about his overall achievement. Yeats is difficult for a number of reasons. Firstly, his work is so varied that he cannot readily be 'sampled'. Secondly, his dialectical mode of thinking resists the reassurance of the handy summary. Thirdly, the course of his development as a writer, spanning as it does the 19th and the 20th centuries, is never easy to plot. Fourthly, with its strange mythology, unfamiliar history, and often unpronounceable names, his work often seems remote to non-Irish readers.

It is remarkable that Yeats criticism has proceeded from an occasionally surprising ignorance not only of the subject himself but also of the status of the primary texts. We are still awaiting the definitive biography, the definitive collection of his letters, and, if one is possible, the definitive edition of his poems. Hone's biography (1942), Wade's *Letters* (*L*, 1954), the *Collected Poems* (*CP*) of 1950 or the more recent edition of *The Poems: A New Edition* (*PNE*) by Finneran (1984), are all for different reasons flawed. Future readers of Yeats, especially when they possess what should be the definitive works, will marvel both at our ignorance and our achievement. Formerly, in the 1930s, when Yeats made his entry into the Anglo-American academy, or in the 1960s, when his greatness was confirmed, criticism and scholarship went hand in hand. Today, especially in the light of deconstructive readings and textual uncertainties, the critic needs to tread more warily.

Biographies of Yeats

Biographical studies of Yeats normally start with Hone (1942), and continue with Ellmann (1948) and Jeffares (1949) – although the latter has now been superseded by Jeffares (1988). Hone's biography relies on a mixture of chronology, the public record, Yeats' letters and poems, and personal reminiscence, but the subject himself remains a distant and largely unexplained figure. This is not a psychological study, and, with Mrs Yeats still alive, Hone was obviously reluctant to explore issues or to divulge personal material; on the question of Yeats' relationships with women, for example, he refuses, as does Jeffares (1949), to identify 'Diana Vernon', the woman Yeats lived with in 1895-6. Added to this is his often cursory treatment of key figures and episodes: for more information on Yeats, the student must seek out other inquiries. Murphy's brief account of the Yeats and Pollexfen families (1971), together with his distinguished biography of Yeats' father (1979), counteracts the impression given by Yeats in *Reveries over Childhood and Youth* (*R*) that his father was cruel and tyrannical. The period immediately following Yeats' marriage in October 1917 is now well documented in Harper (1987), a highly readable and revealing account about the making of *A Vision* (*AV*). Nietzsche's influence and the episode in the winter of 1913-14 when Yeats and Pound were at Stone Cottage are briefly mentioned by Hone. The links between Yeats and these two figures have been extensively explored since; in the case of Nietzsche, by Thatcher (1970), Bridgwater (1972), O'Brien (1975), Bohlmann (1982); in the case of Pound, by Ellmann (1970), Diggory (1983), Litz (1985), and Longenbach (1988). New light on Yeats has also come from studies of less well-known figures, such as Yeats' American patron John Quinn (see Reid, 1968; Himber, 1983) or Yeats' occult friend W.T. Horton (see Harper, 1980).

Ellmann's biography, which concentrates on the development of Yeats' mind, has fared better, in part no doubt because the New Criticism, which sought to keep biography separate from criticism, has gone out of fashion. Ellmann stresses the son's struggle with the father and how his chief defence against the sceptical father was religion. It is a story of Yeats' attempt to find Unity of Being, to integrate the different sides of his personality and the different activities and interests of his life. Hence the emphasis on the Mask, the bifurcated self, the struggle for unity, and the need for new divisions. Ellmann unfolds a compelling psychological drama that draws together Yeats' various interests – nationalist, occult, and literary – into an observable whole. In his search for a more concrete style, in his disillusionment with Ireland, in his spiritual quest, Yeats emerges as a restless pursuer of reality, caught up in a dialectical process that resisted final synthesis.

Jeffares' biography, where the relationship between 'Man' and 'Poet' remains for the most part unaddressed, is less insightful. At one point we are told that 'during these years of excitement, of preoccupation with love and the literary revival, Yeats was publishing steadily'; at another that in *The Countess Kathleen* (*CK*) Yeats is Kevin and Maud Gonne Kathleen. The reader expects more from a biography than lame juxtaposition and simple equivalents. What is missing from Jeffares, especially noticeable after reading Ellmann, is an analysis of how the man and the poet are related. Jeffares' more recent biography (1988), illustrated with contemporary photographs, is a fuller account which brings together information currently scattered elsewhere. The chapter headings are divided by year, but the continuity achieved by this is perhaps too external to do justice to the many strands that weave their way through Yeats' life. Until the new biography by Roy Foster is published, Jeffares' 'territorial' study provides the most up-to-date and authoritative survey. Tuohy's biography (1976), a contextual rather than a psychological study, is one I often recommend to students. The first chapter on Yeats and 19th-century Ireland – significantly not on the family – is an excellent summary of the historical and cultural contexts into which Yeats was born. Non-Irish readers, especially, will welcome his succinct treatment of the significance of Daniel O'Connell and Catholic Emancipation, Thomas Davis and the Nation poets, James Clarence Mangan, the Great Famine of 1845-7, the Catholic Church and Cardinal Cullen, the Fenians and the Irish Republican Brotherhood. Tuohy continues with chapters on Yeats' childhood and youth, the London years of 1887-91, the poets' clubs and secret societies, the Irish theatre and nationalist politics, Coole Park and London society, the Easter Rebellion and the Irish Free State, the Blue Shirts and historical cycles, and finally a chapter on his old age. Particularly through such pairings – the theatre *and* politics, Coole Park *and* London – a portrait emerges of Yeats that is both suggestive and full.

There are numerous recollections which add to our picture of Yeats. In Mikhail (1977) can be found extracts and interviews with those who knew Yeats: Eglinton's memory of him at High School in Dublin; Rhys' recollection of Yeats at the Rhymers' Club and how Yeats was 'the best reader among the Rhymers'; O'Casey's account of Yeats' defence in 1926 of *The Plough and the Stars* and how 'friendship with Yeats was something Sean couldn't reach yet'. Gibbon (1959) contains a view of Yeats in the 1920s and 1930s, his Monday evenings at home which 'had an aristocratic touch', and how Yeats 'had no wish to speak poetry apologetically as though it were prose'. The volume I particularly like is Gwynn (1940), which is lively, unsentimental, and generous in its praise for the poet who had just died. It contains recollections by, among others, Maud Gonne, William Rothenstein, C.Day Lewis, and L.A.G. Strong. 'Without Yeats,' Maud Gonne writes, 'there would have been no Literary Revival in Ireland. Without the inspiration of that Revival and the glorification of beauty and heroic virtue, I doubt if there would have been an Easter Week.' For Strong, Yeats, whose 'terrific sense of reality' lies at the basis of all his work, was 'the greatest poet of his time because he was the most ruthless, the artist who gave everything to his art'. Lady Gregory's *Journals* (1978, 1987), which cover the period from 1916 until her death in 1932, also add to our knowledge of Yeats, as does Gogarty's autobiography (1937). A less flattering picture can be found in

Moore (1911-14), perhaps the most famous autobiography of the Irish Literary revival and the one that Yeats effectively 'answered' in *Dramatis Personae*. Portraits of Yeats in fiction can be found in Moore's *Evelyn Innes* (1898) (as Ulick/Alick, the mage-musician), in AE's (George Russell) *The Interpreters* (1922) (as Lavelle, 'the imperialist of idealism'), and in Aleister Crowley's *Moonchild: A Prologue* (1929) (as Gates).

Introductory Studies

Peterson's introductory study (1982), which takes its bearings from the pioneering work of Kenner (1955), Unterecker (1959), Grossman (1969) and Bradford (1965), can be recommended for anyone studying Yeats for the first time. In his preface he summarises the course of Yeats' career: the 'early search for dreaming wisdom, his difficult transition to a more vigorous and responsible poetry, his mature vision of the power of art and the imagination, and his final rage against old age and death'. Peterson follows Yeats in declaring that the great theme of his poetry as a whole is the clash between Oisin and Patrick. This concern with the larger pattern, whether of theme, sequence, structure or ordering, is the hallmark of this study. Thus in his discussion of Yeats' early volumes Peterson notices how the conflict between dreams and reality in 'The Rose' gives way to the unfulfilled desire of *The Wind Among the Reeds* (*WR*, 1899) and the growing intellectual interest in symbolism. Then come the 'transitional poems' of *In the Seven Woods* (1904) and *The Green Helmet* (*GH*, 1910), when a more realistic mood enters Yeats' verse as a consequence of the final loss of Maud Gonne and of his involvement in the theatre – in 1903 Maud married John MacBride, while in 1904 Yeats became a co-director with Synge and Lady Gregory of the newly-formed Abbey Theatre. In *Responsibilities* (1914) and *The Wild Swans at Coole* (*WSC*, 1917) Yeats comes to accept obligations, while at the same time searching for a new personality. Throughout, Peterson takes care to stress not only the connections between the volumes under discussion but also the dates and the changes in composition of individual poems. In *Michael Robartes and the Dancer* (1921), Peterson groups the poems sequentially – the marriage-bed poems, Easter 1916, poetic wisdom, shocking wisdom – and notes how the volume concludes with the quieter poems. His discussion of *AV* is brisk and to the point, and includes a readable synopsis, an outline of the changes between the 1925/6 and the 1937 editions, and critical reaction. In the same chapter he suggests that *The Winding Stair* (*WS*, 1933) is a counterpoint, a reaction to *The Tower* (*T*,1928) – again, a fertile idea for students to develop on their own or possibly with further help from Faulkner (1987). In the final chapter Peterson considers the last poems and plays together for the light they shed on each other. This study is distinguished by its clarity of style, an interested mind, and a sharp focus on pattern both within the volumes of verse and between one volume and another.

Unterecker's *Guide* (1959) begins with a discussion of the major themes of Yeats' verse – his use of biography, the Mask, occult and visionary systems, images, metaphors, and literary symbols. Unterecker's use of the word 'themes' is unfortunate, since these elements represent not so much themes as techniques or methods for approaching certain themes. However, his detailed comments on the specific volumes and on individual poems remain an indispensable starting-point for students. He shows, for example, how the imagery of birds and trees in *WO* is not merely decorative but contributes to the poem's structure, how the function of symbols is more important than the paraphrasable meaning. In *WR*, Unterecker argues, Yeats is concerned not with the representation of reality but with constructing a 'vision of reality'. *In The Seven Woods* (1903) is marked by 'dramatised conversation', while in *GH* a pair of uncontroversial public poems frame a set of increasingly arrogant and highly personal lyrics. *Responsibilities* marks a plateau of reappraisal and renewal. In his discussion of *WSC*, Unterecker provides a fine exposition of its interconnectedness and traces the movement from the anecdotal poems on Robert Gregory's death through the formal elegy, the Mask poems, the studies of love and death, and onto the early formulation of the new System. Throughout, he concentrates on the interrelatedness of Yeats' verse. Thus, *T* finds its complement in *WS*, the male giving way to the female, the stress on bitterness and the sterility of Ireland to a hopeful mood of regeneration and affirmation. Although some comments, such as his account of the order of *Last Poems* (*LP*), are not wholly reliable, this guide is still valuable, not least in enabling students to gain a purchase on

Yeats' verse simply by seeing how one poem and one volume shape up against another.

A more advanced introduction to several crucial aspects of Yeats can be found in Gordon (1961). Based on an exhibition of paintings and illustrative material held in 1960, this book draws attention to the visual arts in Yeats' life and work, for Yeats was after all, as he reminded an audience in 1910, 'a painter's son' (see O'Driscoll and Reynolds, 1975). The first of five sections deals in an original way with the portraits and physical appearance of Yeats, with the way changes here reflect changes in the poet himself, and how the black of the Twilight era gave way to coloured tweeds, green or blue shirts in later life. The second section on 'Persons and Places' explores the Irish dimension and the places in the West that feature in his work – Coole Park and Ballylee, Lissadell and Sligo. 'Poet and Theatre' concentrates on three phases – the Bedford Park years of 1887-91 when Yeats developed an interest in a new form of drama, the period round the turn of the century when a national theatre in Ireland was created, and a third phase, particularly associated with *At the Hawk's Well* (*ATHW*, 1916), when Yeats became interested in Japanese Noh drama. Then follows an illuminating discussion of Yeats' concept of Byzantium, how it differed from the late 19th-century view of Byzantine culture and history, and how it was incorporated into his work by Yeats' synthetic method. The fourth section on 'Symbolic Art and Visionary Landscape' outlines Yeats' taste in painting and includes reference to the Pre- Raphaelites, the idea of art as image, his concern for pattern and rhythm, the important distinction between allegory and symbol, and his abiding interest in the work of Blake, Palmer, and Calvert. A final section by Kermode on 'The Dancer' reminds us – even if the connection is not made explicitly by the contributors – that London and Paris are also part of the 'People and Places' of Yeats' world. This book wears its learning with ease; it is especially good on the late 19th-century Victorian background, but is less so on the middle and later Yeats, who is for the most part absent.

Archibald (1983) can also be recommended at this stage, especially for the unobtrusive yet authoritative way in which he lays the groundwork for a study of Yeats' verse. His concern is to emphasise Yeats' 'imaginative growth and the many and various attempts to achieve a personal history, a realised self and a completed *oeuvre'*. His first chapter distinguishes Yeats and Coleridge as Romantic poets: Coleridge has a belief in the possibility of discovery, while Yeats is less sure and and 'searches for assertion without belief, assurance without doctrine, conviction without dogma'. Subsequent chapters trace Yeats' relationship with his father, with friends such as Mabel Beardsley, Maud Gonne and Lady Gregory, analyse Yeats' changing views of Ireland before and after 1913, and provide an outline of *A Vision* (*AV*) together with a four-point list of the creed to which *AV* subscribes. Throughout, Archibald attends to specific poems and he writes well about *WO*, *T* and the 'Byzantium' poems. He concludes with a discussion of *LP* and Yeats' shifting final statements, which, being at once more intense, vulnerable and honest, refuse 'the Grand Statement'.

Bibliographical Details

For bibliographical information, the place to start is Wade's third edition (1968), which lists not only publication details of the various editions of Yeats' texts but also a summary of contents, order and first appearance. This is indispensable for deconstructing the later editions and anthologies and for reassembling or reconstructing Yeats. Cross and Dunlop (1971) is still useful up to 1965, though it needs to be supplemented by reference to the more intimidating Jochum (1978), which is 'reasonably complete through 1971'. Information about more recent titles can be found in Finneran (1976) and Finneran (1983a), in the *Yeats Annual* (1982-), and in *Yeats: An Annual of Critical and Textual Studies* (1983-). There are separate concordances for the verse and drama, edited respectively by Parrish and Painter (1963) and Domville (1972). Jeffares has produced two invaluable guides, one with Knowland on the plays (1975), the other on the poems (1984), and these can be augmented by Saul (1957 and 1958). The Jeffares guides provide information about sources, dates of composition, place of publication, relevant biographical details, help with interpreting complex images or obscure references, as well as comments by critics.

A discerning second-hand bookseller will have a copy of Wade to verify a first edition Yeats, but checking on Yeats is no easy task. There are more than 366 entries in Wade of books by Yeats, of books edited or with prefaces by him, and books to which he contributed; and, as if to further complicate matters, Yeats constantly revised his work and published it in as many trade editions as he could. The best way to read Yeats' verse is in a first edition, for here there are no revisions, re-orderings, omissions, or deletions, and, at least in one sense, no corruption – though bear in mind the differing dates of composition and first appearance of individual poems. Most students have to rely on subsequent editions, not all of which, as we shall see in the next chapter, are reliable. But the best approach is to return to the first edition, thumb through its pages, notice the designs on the cover and the spine, especially if they are by Sturge Moore or Althea Gyles, mark the layout of the text, and think of the care that has gone into its production as a book. Other elementary mistakes can be prevented. You will look in vain, for example, for a first edition of 'Crossways' or 'The Rose', for these volumes are the insertions by Yeats into later collected editions. Other insights emerge from such editions. The 1908 date of the first Collected edition is intriguing, and prompts the thought that perhaps Yeats believed his life's work was drawing to a close, in which case he would, arguably, be of only minor interest to us today.

Most readers do not have access to first editions, though it is by no means rare to find copies of *T* and *WS* on open shelves in university and college libraries. Next best are copies of the *Variorum* editions of the poems and the plays (1957 and 1966 respectively), which list the major changes between first and subsequent versions. For the more advanced student none of these changes can be ignored, even if they involve Yeats' seemingly erratic use of what some critics refer to as 'rhetorical punctuation', while for those studying Yeats for the first time the changes in the 1892 and subsequent versions of *CK* can serve to highlight the importance of textual revision in Yeats and the need to be clear which version is under discussion. *CP* and *CPI* are the most widely available texts, but these do not include variants, and the status of the former, especially since the publication of *The Poems: A New Edition*, has recently been the subject of heated exchanges.

The path to Yeats' prose writings has also not been trouble-free. *Mythologies* (*M*, 1959) brings together *The Celtic Twilight* (*CT*, 1893), *The Secret Rose* (*SR*, 1897), *Stories of Red*

Hanrahan (1897), *Rosa Alchemica, The Tables of the Law, and the Adoration of the Magi* (1897) and *Per Amica Silentia Lunae* (*PASL*, 1918), but this can be confusing for students, and this for several reasons. Yeats never wrote a book entitled 'Mythologies', and, in spite of its being based on *Early Poems and Stories* (1925), it is not altogether clear, *pace* Schricker (1982), how all these separate books belong together under this awkward title. *CT*, for example, consists of folk material that Yeats collected from the country people round Sligo; the Hanrahan stories, based as they are on an 18th-century figure called Owen Rua O'Sullivan, owe much to the oral tradition of storytelling; the stories in *SR* and the following three stories are visionary tales combining elements of history, autobiography and symbolism that take as part of their theme the war between heaven and earth; *PASL* is discursive, not narrative prose, and expounds Yeats' new ideas about character and personality, the Primary and the Antithetical self, the vocabulary that belongs in other words more appropriately to a discussion of *AV*. Moreover, the editions referred to on the Contents page are not strictly accurate: the anthology does not use the 1893 edition of *CT* but for the most part the revised edition of 1902; although six Hanrahan stories were included in *SR* 1897, *Stories of Red Hanrahan* as a separate volume was first published not in 1897 but in 1904; *The Secret Rose* in *M* is not from the 1897 edition, for this began with a story entitled 'The Binding of the Hair' and ended with 'Rosa Alchemica'; and no book was ever published entitled'Rosa Alchemica, The Tables of the Law, and The Adoration of the Magi'. Fortunately, the deficiences outlined here have been partly rectified by the recent issue of *The Secret Rose And Other Stories* (1988), for this includes the more sensible arrangement of *CT*, *SR*, and *Stories of Red Hanrahan*.

Yeats as storyteller would have been better served if an anthology had been produced that included 'Dhoya' (1887), his first story, *John Sherman* (1891), his intriguing first novel, the stories in *CT* (1893) and *SR* (1897) with an account of their subsequent revisions, *The Tables of the Law and The Adoration of the Magi*, together with *The Speckled Bird*, which was not published until 1976 even though it is arguably the most compelling autobiographical account we have of Yeats in the crucial years between 1896 and 1902. Such an anthology would remind us of several things: Yeats' strong, early interest in the genre; how story-telling connects with his work as a collector of folklore material and as an anthologist of Irish literature; how he was always experimental, restlessly searching for the most appropriate form; how, in his attempt to combine aspects of an oral tradition, he refused to accept the known or more conventional kinds of storytelling; and how fiction laid the groundwork for the poetry and drama to come.

Essays and Introductions (*E & I*, 1961), a collection of Yeats' literary criticism to be found for the most part in *Ideas of Good and Evil* (1903), *The Cutting of an Agate* (1912) and in *Essays, 1931 to 1936* (1937), is less problematic, largely because of its more unified design. *Explorations* (*Ex*, 1962) is, as its title permits, a mixed bag: introductions to works on folklore and mythology by Lady Gregory (which more properly belong with *M*); articles and essays on plays, especially in the period from 1901 to 1908; the 1919 reflective essay 'If I Were Four-and-Twenty', which includes the famous sentence 'Hammer your thoughts into unity'; 'Pages From A Diary Written in Nineteen Hundred and Thirty'; introductions to four of his middle/late plays; and the polemic on Ireland, civilisation, and eugenics, to be found in *On the Boiler* (1939). It is difficult to know what is being explored here. Leaving aside *Autobiographies* (*A*), which will be discussed more fully in chapter 4, and the two *Uncollected Prose* anthologies (Yeats, 1970b and Yeats, 1975), Yeats' other major prose work *AV* is now available in two editions. There is the second edition of 1937 (*AVB*), which is the basis of the standard trade edition, and there is the first edition of 1925/6 (*AVA*), which has recently been reissued under the editorship of Harper and Hood (1978), and the differences between the two editions are not without interest for anyone investigating the changes in Yeats' 'stylistic arrangement of experience' from the 1920s to the 1930s.

Yeats' texts are currently being republished by Macmillan in a Collected Edition, which will significantly reshape our picture of his work. Equally promising is the new Penguin series, under the general editorship of Timothy Webb, of annotated editions of Yeats' fiction, *A*, folklore, drama and poetry, materials on politics and Irish literature, and essays on literature and art. The Cornell Yeats, a series devoted to manuscript materials, began in 1982 with *DC* edited by Marcus (1982), and has continued with *Purgatory* edited by Siegel (1984), and *Volume One of The Early Poetry* containing the MS materials for *Mosada* and *The Island of*

Statues edited by Bornstein (1987). Colin Smythe is working on a revision to Wade's *Bibliography*, while Wade's *Letters* (*L*, 1954) are now being superseded by the publication of *The Collected Letters* (*CL*, 1985-). *A Descriptive Catalog of W.B. Yeats' Library* has been handsomely produced by Garland Publishing (1985). New biographies of Yeats by Roy Foster and of George Yeats by Ann Saddlemyer are promised and should yield new insights. All this reflects a growing desire on the part of Yeats scholars to provide ready access to the necessary information for critical judgments. It is to be hoped that the ground is being prepared for a new awakening in Yeats criticism.

Chapter 2

Yeats' Poetry

The Process of Composition

A significant impact on Yeats studies has been made by critics examining the various drafts of Yeats' work. Brooks and Warren (1938) and Brooks (1939), who as New Critics were committed to the principle of a text or poem's autonomy, discovered, however, when faced with explicating Yeats' verse, the need to refer to Yeats' prose works and in particular to the account of his system in *AV*. Other critics, such as Parkinson (1951 and 1964), remind us that New Criticism would also have benefitted from a closer scrutiny of Yeats' drafts and revisions. In a series of articles written in the late 1940s (see Cross and Dunlop), as well as in his biography of 1949, Jeffares made use of unpublished material, held for the most part by Mrs Yeats and by the National Library of Ireland in Dublin. This material has continued to be mined by scholars in the post-war period, and it would have been helpful had it been made more widely available. The diary entries of 1908-13, for example, which are especially relevant for a fuller understanding of *A*, were not published until 1972. The publication of the entire extant drafts for the poems, however, largely because of the size of the undertaking, has never been seriously contemplated. So, without the manuscripts to hand, the student must rely on the various selections that have appeared in different critical works in the last 40 years, on Wade (1968) and Ellmann (1954) for a chronology of the composition of the poems, and on Ellmann's partial and incomplete Appendix 'Towards a Reading of the Poems' in (1954). Here in this section I concentrate on the work of Parkinson (1951 and 1964), Bradford (1965), Stallworthy (1963 and 1969), and Clark (1983).

Parkinson's two books on the process of composition, in which he argues for the significance of Yeats' involvement in the Abbey Theatre and how this transformed the nature of his poetry, are complementary. In the first volume (1951) he considers the revisions to Yeats' early poetry, in the second (1964) the composition of the later verse. The distinguishing feature of both is that he places a discussion of revisions within a larger framework of interpretation. The first book begins with an examination of the poems in 'The Rose' and 'Crossways' and of the poems in *WO* (1889) that Yeats revised or excluded from *Poems* (1895). The work excluded defines Yeats in 1895, and other revisions reveal a poet increasingly immersed in a Celtic world, which was simultaneously drawing closer to his own time and place. Citing the revisions made to 'The Madness of King Goll' and 'The Indian to his Love', Parkinson underlines how Yeats' verse becomes simpler, less pretentious, how he uses a more natural syntax with fewer inversions and discards 'thou', how his words are more suggestive and at the same time more specific. By *WR* (1899) – the culmination of his early lyric style – his subject-matter is primarily Irish, and more emphasis is given to speech, but Parkinson is quick to remind us (in line with his overall argument) that Yeats' rhapsodic style is limited, unable to handle more than one aspect of human experience, and in need of dramatic conflict and moments of 'passionate intensity'.

Between 1899 and 1911 Yeats wrote a play a year, and learnt in the process how to become a dramatic poet. The changes between the 1900 and the 1905 version of *The Shadowy Waters* (*SW*) embody a stronger sense of dramatic purpose, especially evident in the area of conflict, in the development of character, in the more natural syntax and diction, and in the deployment of a less esoteric symbolism. *On Baile's Strand* (1907) and other plays written at this time reminded Yeats of the necessary existence of the circumstantial world, forcing him to reconsider his entire poetic practice. A new mode of self-dramatisation is evident in *In the Seven Woods* (1903), but this is still tentative – between 1903 and 1908 Yeats wrote only four lyrics that he cared to print in the *Collected Works* of 1908. Thereafter, his lyric production increased, and *GH* (1910) displays a poet responding more vigorously than before to the demands of the immediate world. Personal speech now has the look of dramatised tension, and he seeks a relationship between a daily mood and a moment of exaltation. This is especially evident in the poems surrounding the Hugh Lane controversy, such as 'September 1913', 'To a Friend', and 'Paudeen'. From *WSC* (1917), *Michael Robartes and the*

Dancer (1921), and onwards into his later verse, Yeats shows how he had learnt to subordinate his rhapsodic and ecstatic impulses to the demands of structure and situation. As to the changes Yeats made to his early verse in 1925-33, Parkinson makes the following observations. He insists, for example, that his study highlights not the discontinuity but the continuity of the early and later Yeats, and that there is an inherent tendency in Yeats towards conflict which his involvement with drama brought out. The common element in his poetry, in evidence both before and after 1901, is 'formal passionate speech', though after 1901 this becomes more eloquent and has more to communicate. The theatre enabled Yeats to recognise the importance of the moment of passion and how the daily world could be transfigured, and this in turn lent to his middle and later verse a dramatic structure. Parkinson also maintains that changes made to his earlier verse, sometimes motivated by a change of outlook, sometimes for technical considerations, illustrate the interdependence of attitude and technique, how often in origin a change could be technical but in effect substantial.

Parkinson's main argument that Yeats' poetry is largely determined by his dramatic sense is expanded in (1964). He refers briefly to the presentation of the self in Eliot and Pound, the general issue of sincerity in writing, and the relationship between maker and artifact. He then addresses the issue of Yeats' search for a role, a means to transcend the daily self, and embody the truth. The poet, he suggests, has five modes available to him: the individuated person whose life gives weight to his words; the social character, the site of tension between a social and a personal identity ('Dialogue of Self and Soul', 'Vacillation'); the poet as prophet revealing truth ('Among School Children'); the poet as overt dramatist adopting a persona (the Crazy Jane sequence); the poet as editor and maker of books. Parkinson suggests that the crucial year in Yeats' development is 1917. After this date, Yeats' career enters another phase, beginning with an act of purification in *A* and an act of elaboration in *AVA*, and distinguished from the first phase by his ability to view his knowledge and experience as not his own.

Parkinson's second chapter examines Yeats' methods of composition, the gap between draft and poem, and the various kinds of gestation in the emergence of a poem. This took many forms: the embodiment of an idea, the exploration of a feeling, the contemplation of an icon, the fascination with the simple rhythm of a phrase that proclaimed a mood in need of either rebuke or acceptance. For his examples Parkinson takes 'After Long Silence' and 'Among School Children'. The drafts of the latter poem illustrate how in the course of writing Yeats changed direction, moving away from self-pity and complaint towards revelation and exultation: Parkinson's discussion is especially revealing at this point. In his third chapter Parkinson disputes the allegorical view of Yeats as proposed by Wilson (1958) and sides more with Kermode's (1957) belief, that a Yeats poem is a unique symbol, is its own context, and cannot be read in terms of some perennial philosophy. Citing the symbol of the swan in Yeats' verse, Parkinson also takes issue with Stauffer (1949), and suggests that Yeats' verse is primarily dramatic and not composed of symbols. There is no settled pattern of association, and it is merely confusing, for example, to identify the swan in 'Leda and the Swan' with the swan in 'Among School Children'.

Parkinson's fourth chapter on Yeats' passionate syntax is also penetrating, informative and persuasive. He reveals how Yeats combined syllabic and stress prosody, how in the more formal poems he used ten syllables per line, while in writing more intense lyrics he tended to employ a fixed number of stresses. Some of Yeats' prosody, such as that to be found in 'Crazy Jane and the Journeyman', is highly complicated, but this has to be understood by reference to the poem's metaphysical structure. *LP* contains more anomalous prosodic features, a fact which Parkinson interprets in the context of Yeats' desire for liberation. He notes, for instance, the parallel with the decline in use of symbols after 1932, as if Yeats were aware that icons could no longer be trusted to carry the burden of a poem's argument. A final, brief chapter on Yeats and post-war American poetry, which includes references to Ginsberg's 'Howl' and Lowell's *Life Studies*, returns us to Parkinson's opening remarks on the presentation of the self in poetry, and he reflects on two facts: firstly, that Yeats' influence has been less than one might suppose, considering his stature as the greatest poet of the first half of the 20th century, and, secondly, that he seems out of place in the context of modern poetry. Parkinson's work is not the only benchmark to assess the contribution of other critics to the study of Yeats' drafts and revisions, but it does affirm the value of hermeneutics and a theory of interpretation; the study of drafts and revisions requires a discerning as well as a deciphering eye.

Bradford (1965) outlines the process of composition to be found in Yeats' poems, plays and prose. This, too, is an informative book which keeps in mind the student who does not have access to the MSS. Bradford tells us, for example, that before 1917 Yeats wrote in cheap exercise books, while after his marriage he used looseleaf notebooks which could be rearranged. He wrote on the right-hand side, keeping the left page for revisions. If he was happy with what he had written he would sign and date it. In his introduction to the poems, Bradford makes a number of general observations on Yeats' varied practice. Yeats almost always began work on a poem by composing a sketch or subject in prose, from which Bradford draws a number of tentative conclusions. Yeats wrote about subjects at various stages of his meditating on a poem; the close relationship of sketch and poem does not indicate that Yeats found the writing of the poem easy ('Coole Park, 1929' was difficult to compose, 'Byzantium' easy); the subjects themselves do not indicate whether Yeats is recording a major or a minor inspiration. Bradford also notices that the drafts of a poem are sometimes ahead of the form; sometimes stanzas were written in a different order – stanza V was probably the first stanza of 'Among School Children' to be composed; Yeats often chose a rhyme word or sound to 'block out' or give shape to a stanza; and he used rhetorical rather than grammatical punctuation, hearing pauses at the end of lines.

General observations on Yeats' practice inevitably give way to an account of the changes from the early to the later Yeats. In this respect Bradford compares and contrasts *WR* with the later verse. In *WR* the principal effort is to write the poem in a single sentence, to make the poetic and grammatical unit coincide; Yeats has not yet achieved the metaphysical penetration of his later verse. He has not yet mastered a form or a diction suited to a poem such as 'Byzantium'; nor has he begun to invent the forceful *personae* of his later verse. What Yeats lacks here is summed up by Bradford in the phrase 'personal utterance' (a phrase first used by Yeats in March 1910), and here Bradford follows Parkinson's stress on drama. The idea of personal utterance is traced from *WSC*, a volume where Yeats writes about his life as something intended, complete, achieved, through the poems in the 1920s where the prevailing mode is public speech, and onto the metaphysical reflection expressed in the poems of the 1930s. Bradford's study tends to foreground the problem of transcription, and is less coherent than Parkinson, but as a source book for a study of the poems, plays, or prose, it should not be neglected.

The discussion of particular poems in Stallworthy's two books (1963 and 1969) is detailed and often perceptive, but his general remarks have lasted less well. In (1963) he examines 18 poems including the 'Byzantium' poems, 'The Second Coming', the 1892 and 1925 versions of 'The Sorrow of Love', and 'The Black Tower', and comes to the following rather unexceptional conclusions: there is a strong structural sense both in the finished poem and in stanza-building; Yeats experimented in later years with half-rhymes (Parkinson (1964) observes – more correctly – that off-rhymes, 'the world of divided imperfection', became prevalent after 1903); the typical poetic movement is from the personal to the general; more than any other English poet, Yeats wrote about individual people; his work is both retrospective and apocalyptic and he has a 'razor-sharp self-critical faculty'. Knowledge of the drafts can prevent misreadings, clarify difficulties and highlight intention. To this extent it is of value to know, for example, that Burke and the Russian Revolution were in Yeats' mind when he was composing 'The Second Coming', or that behind 'The Black Tower', a poem written a week before his death in January 1939, there stands perhaps the figure of Hitler. But equally what Stallworthy's study illustrates is how the history of Yeats criticism is not unlike a partial, hesitant discovery of the orginal MSS. Stallworthy's second book, which concentrates on *LP*, is more coherent, though the opening two chapters on 'The Dynastic Theme' and 'The Prophetic Voice', which are designed to orientate the reader to the major concerns of that volume, are too vague to be of real use. The dynastic theme, for example, surfaces in Yeats in the decade or so after 1908: by *LP* its association with race and eugenics has turned it into something less gentle. Similarly, when Stallworthy compares *LP* with *T* and *WSC* and suggests that Yeats is now anxious to speak out because his time is short, he fails to observe: that *T*, if anything, is his testamentary volume; that *LP* has the voice not so much of the prophet as of someone beyond the grave; that, arguably, 'Politics' is as fitting a conclusion to his poetic career as 'Under Ben Bulben'; and that *LP* is more provisional than its title might suggest.

Clark's study (1983) concentrates on poems written between 1926 and 1931. He prepares the reader by suggesting that the best editors are those who pay attention not just to the words on the page but also to their context. The contexts that Clark invokes are the most far-reaching of any of the critics considered here, for Clark is like a detective probing the authority of known accounts and sifting anew the evidence presented by the MSS themselves. He informs us, for example, that the path from draft to final poem sometimes involves an inquiry not simply into the MSS but also into paintings, other literary sources, or other Yeats poems. In his discussion of 'Three Things' Clark notices that the phrase 'stretch and yawn' is not an image of sexual consummation but of arousal, that the phrase echoes Pound's 'yawn and stretch', which first appeared in *The Spirit of Romance* (1910), and that in the drafts stanza three is an afterthought. The woman in 'After Long Silence' is identified by Ellmann and Parkinson as Olivia Shakespear, but Clark, in reviewing the evidence especially in connection with *AVA* and 'All Souls' Night', concludes that the reconciliation referred to in the poem is not with his former lover but with Mrs Mathers, who had been upset by the portrayal of her husband in *AVA*. Taking issue with Parkinson, and picking up on an unnoticed colon that appears after the word 'song' in some of the drafts, Clark also claims that it is not love which is the supreme theme but bodily decrepitude. In his discussion of the dragon in *Michael Robartes and the Dancer* and 'Her Triumph' he shows how the source is to be located not in a painting as Henn (1950) assumes but in a poem by William Morris. An examination of the drafts of 'From the "Antigone"' yields another kind of caution; Yeats used not only the Masqueray translation, as Jeffares (1984) claims, but also Jebb and Lewis Campbell. In spite of its narrow focus on a handful of poems, this study, which has met with a lively response (see, for example, Fletcher, 1985), extends the principles governing an inquiry into Yeats at work. It is a challenging and slightly unnerving account, for even as it sheds new light on familiar poems it makes us conscious of the extent of the darkness that perhaps surrounds the remaining 400 or so Yeats poems not included in Clark's discussion.

The Order of the Poems

'The Sacred Book of the Arts'

Yeats 'didn't accumulate poems, he wrote books'. So declared Kenner (1955) in typically arresting fashion, echoing no doubt Yeats' own prophetic remark that 'one poem lights up another' (*Poems*, 1912, p.xi). Ironically, as an extended argument, Kenner's essay, which tends merely to repeat its original insight, is not impressive, but in the development of Yeats studies it has played a key role. In constructing a volume of poems, Yeats took care to achieve the right balance. 'A Prayer for my Daughter' significantly follows, and qualifies, the noisy, apocalyptic strains of 'The Second Coming'; 'Sailing to Byzantium' acts as an overture to an exploration of the intractability of history and the decline into old age, and the volume concludes with an epilogue written in 1920 entitled 'All Souls' Night'. Yeats' volumes often do not reflect their compositional history, but are ordered in such a way as to suggest their unity. Again, to appreciate this fully, the student of Yeats needs to see a first edition. Equally, as Martin (Donoghue and Mulryne, 1965) cautions in his discussion of *WSC*, the unity of a Yeats volume should not always be assumed and sometimes still has to be defended; in this instance Martin discerns not the unity of the volume but two distinct series of poems. Engelberg (1964), we might notice in passing, goes further and suggests that Yeats' poetry is so various that no one representative theory could support it.

But the influence of Kenner's essay has been profound, and some of the best essays and books on Yeats – as well as more pedestrian ones, such as Young (1987) – have been those which affirm the unity of his texts. The essays by Davie on *Michael Robartes and the Dancer* and by Holloway on *T* in Donoghue and Mulryne (1965), for example, support Kenner's contention. The meaning of 'Easter 1916' is enhanced when read alongside other poems in a collection, while certain repeated rhetorical modes, such as the exhortation to women to avoid abstraction, or a common discursive style, reinforce the unity of the volume. In terms of full-length studies which stress unity, Grossman's reading (1969) of *WR* is in many ways the best. This is an ambitious, intelligent, difficult, but largely sustained account of Yeats' transformation in the 1890s. Eschewing the conventional view of

Yeats' escapism, Grossman traces the poet's desire for Wisdom (or, we might say, the Muse) and his fear that this is unattainable. *WR*, whose basic myth is the encounter between the suitor of the absolute and its symbol, the Wisdom figure, cultivates the unattainable: the suitor undergoes an experience of the *mysterium tremendum*; this brings not happiness but the realisation that Wisdom feeds malignantly on his life.

WR is faithful to the temporal sequence not only in terms of composition and biography but also in the way it reflects the whole development of Celticism in the 1890s. Thus eight of the first twelve poems were written before 1894, are genetically heterogeneous, and exhibit a mixture of styles that bear traces of the 'ossianic', moments of trance, the aesthetic movement, Morris, and the living style that Yeats was fashioning for himself. The second section of poems, the next thirteen, beginning with 'Aedh Laments the Loss of Love' through to 'Aedh Tells of the Perfect Beauty', are dominated by the white woman, and were composed around 1896. This is the period of Yeats' writing for *The Savoy*, of his affair with Olivia Shakespear and of his associated fear and recoil. The third section, the final twelve poems, where the primary relationship is to an unbodied ideal and the impulse is to free himself from emotion, foreshadows, with its complex philosophical thought and use of intellectual symbols, the later poetry. In a wide-ranging and rewarding discussion, Grossman underlines the unity of the volume. He refers to the symbols, the moods, the discourse on war and apocalypse, the use of Aedh, Hanrahan and Michael Robartes to represent one kind of persona while Aherne, Finivarach and Mongan embody another.

Murphy (1975) and Putzel (1986) have followed Grossman in writing full-length studies of Yeats' early work. Murphy is less convinced that *WR* embodies the search for poetic knowledge or that the apocalypse can be equated with the imagination; for him the volume represents 'a collapse into destructive vision'. Putzel, on the other hand, builds on Grossman's account and not only stresses the unity of *WR* but also makes out a good case for seeing *WR* and *SR* as companion volumes. Thus, both texts articulate tensions between the diachronic and synchronic planes, both contain similar themes of time, love, and apocalypse, and *WR* 'presents the "liturgy" of the symbolic system as outlined in SR'. Arguing for the unity of a volume can lead to distortion, exaggeration, and an occasionally irritating metalanguage, but in these recent studies this is largely offset by the new awareness gained.

The Finneran debate
In an uncanny coincidence Yeats and Joyce studies were thrown into some disarray by the publication within twelve months of each other in 1983 and 1984 of Finneran's *W.B. Yeats: The Poems* (*PNE*) and Gabler's edition of *Ulysses*. As I write, the outcome of both disputes remains unsettled, and, although from the outside it might be fun to see the sparks fly, the conflict can have only a deleterious effect for tutors and students, not least in the uncertainty as to which edition to recommend or buy. Gabler's difficulties with Joyce scholars would have been eased if his edition didn't carry the *imprimatur* inherent in the phrase 'The Corrected Text'; Finneran (or his publisher Macmillan) would have been better advised not to jump to conclusions or claim, in the words of the dust jacket, that this is 'the authorised arrangement' or that this edition represents 'all the poems intended for publication by Yeats'. For Yeatsians and Joyceans, protective perhaps of their battered old copies, both recognise the provisional nature of the texts involved. With *Ulysses*, the editorial problems revolve round the status of previous editions and corrections made to the various stages of the MSS. With Yeats, if we leave aside the issue of whether it was appropriate to print all of Yeats' poems – even the ones he had discarded – the issue has focused in particular on the change in the order of *LP* (*PNE*), an issue which is superficially much larger than the corresponding Joyce dispute but which is, I would argue, less fundamental.

Unlike the student of Joyce, the student of Yeats has more than one edition currently in print, so that what is at stake in changes in the order of the poems can quickly be ascertained. In *Collected Poems* (*CP*) the order of *LP* runs from 'The Gyres' to 'Under Ben Bulben'; in *PNE* we find the first section entitled 'New Poems' (*NP*, 1938), a new division inserted after the poem with the appropriate title 'Are You Content?', and a new volume introduced under the title 'Last Poems' (1938-9). The order of *NP* is the same, but *CP* and *PNE* differ in their account of *LP*, which can be briefly summarised as follows: 'Under Ben Bulben' is transferred from the end of *CP* to the beginning of *LP* in *PNE*; 'The Black Tower' is moved from its penultimate position in *CP* and placed third in *LP* (*PNE*); 'Cuchulain Comforted' is removed from its position near the end of *CP* to become the fourth poem in *LP* (*PNE*); 'Hound Voice' changes place with 'John Kinsella's Lament for Mrs Mary Moore'; 'Man and Echo' is promoted ahead of 'The Circus Animals' Desertion' in *LP* (*PNE*); 'Three Marching Songs' is added to *LP* (*PNE*); and three poems – 'Why Should Old Men Not Be Mad', 'The Statesman's Holiday', and 'Crazy Jane on the Mountain' – are relegated to 'Additional Poems' in *PNE*. Probably the most striking change concerns 'Under Ben Bulben' and 'Politics', for in *PNE* these two poems open and close *LP* and thus reshape our view of the volume as a whole. 'Under Ben Bulben' is no longer, as many critics have assumed, a fitting climax to Yeats' life's work, but rather the preface to a volume where all the poems speak to us from beyond the grave, as it were. At the same time the much less assertive poem 'Politics', in contrast with the chill of the epitaph that formerly concluded *CP*, returns us in the end to the human world again.

Finneran defends his decision for this change of order. No edition of Yeats' poems can be definitive he rightly asserts, and he then proceeds to take issue along the lines of 'later and correct' with the two-volumed 1949 chronological edition of Yeats' poems (*PY*). Some of the proofs used in the construction of *PY* date from 1932, while revisions Yeats made to the 1933 *CP* were ignored. The questioning of *PY* began with Bradford (1961), and this was elaborated in his later study (1966). While working on the Yeats papers in Dublin in the summer of 1960 Bradford discovered the MS table of contents for *LP*. Here was proof that Yeats was responsible for the order of poems in *Last Poems and Two Plays* published by the Cuala Press in 1939, and it is this order that Finneran follows in *PNE*.

Part of the difficulty for later editors arises from the fact that Yeats was involved in corrections to three different editions at roughly the same time. In 1930 Macmillan agreed to publish the Edition de Luxe (later known as the Coole Edition), but this was constantly postponed, and, finally, in November 1939 because of the war, 'suspended'. Volume One, which Yeats had got ready in 1931, and the proofs of which he corrected in summer 1932, was to have been devoted to the poems. For whatever reason – Finneran suggests it was as a result of pressure from Yeats who was aggrieved at the delays in publishing the Edition de Luxe – Macmillan agreed in March 1933 to publish a one-volume trade edition of his *Collected Poems* (*CP,* 1933). To make this edition more attractive Macmillan proposed that it open with shorter lyrical poems and that longer narrative ones be placed at the end. Yeats concurred, though it is unclear what implications should be drawn from this. On this matter *PY* reverts to the proofs for the Edition de Luxe and places *WO* first, while Finneran chooses to follow *CP* 1933. In June 1933 Macmillan sent Yeats the proofs of *CP* 1933 and suggested that the section entitled 'The Winding Stair and Other Poems' be published in a separate volume. Proofs for this were ready by August, and in September of the same year *WS* was published. Whenever he has a choice between two readings in that particular part of *PNE*, Finneran prefers the proofs for *WS* over *CP* 1933 . If all this isn't complicated enough, we also need to bear in mind that the principal editor at Macmillan, Thomas Mark, and Yeats' wife George collaborated on an edition of the poetry after Yeats' death. Finneran argues that the defects in *PY* – Mark departs from *CP* 1933 on more than 75 occasions – stem from the decision of Mark and Mrs Yeats to prefer the proofs of the Edition de Luxe over *CP* 1933, thus ignoring the principle of 'later and correct'.

After discussing *A Full Moon in March* (1935) and *NP*, and after justifying the reasons for his differences with *PY*, Finneran then considers *LP*. The table of contents for an untitled volume – presumably *Last Poems and Two Plays* – was composed within two weeks of Yeats' death, and this, Finneran believes, confirms Bradford's conjecture that there is no authority for the order produced by Mark and Mrs Yeats. *PNE* follows this table of contents, as it does with that of *NP* (1938). Finneran also examines changes in punctuation and other emendations to specific lines and poems, and defends his decision to include not only poems which Yeats excluded from his collections but also poems from his plays and elsewhere.

The response of critics to Finneran's edition has been on the whole unfavourable. Montague (1984) dismisses it as 'impressive and risible', adding that 'one of the major contributions of this edition is to clarify Yeats' commas'. Ricks (1984), in a review hostile not only to the edition but to the poet himself, asserts that Yeats knew what he was doing when he excluded the additional poems from his collections of verse. Gould (1984) claims that Finneran has evaded a full examination of the archive and that he has produced something that is 'unsatisfactory in canon, in order, and in text'. On specific criticisms Gould remarks: poems from plays and prose and discarded poems should not be included; it is not clear what kind of edition *PNE* is; Finneran doesn't provide the material for assessing either *PY* or Mark and Mrs Yeats' involvement in *PY*; Finneran is right to restore 'Under Ben Bulben' to the beginning of *LP* (*PNE*) but the chronological ordering of *PY* is preferable to *PNE*; the emendations to 'The Municipal Gallery Revisited' and 'The Bronze Head', to take specific examples, produce bizarre readings; the notes are confusing and Gould refers the reader at this point to the more reliable Jeffares (1975). Donoghue (1984) claims that with its omissions, additions, and misprints, *PNE* is technically 'disastrous'. He agrees with the inclusion of 'Three Songs to the One Burden' but prefers a chronological ordering to the poems. In a review essay, Sidnell (1985) voices similar criticism but provides a more detailed discussion of the issues raised by *PNE*. He supports the idea of a new edition, which will benefit from Finneran's work, but he believes that *PNE* is 'not, overall, an advance over earlier ones...*PNE* merely substitutes Finneran's "feeling" for the text for that of his predecessors'. In conclusion Sidnell asks on what text is Jeffares' *Commentary* now a commentary. Jeffares himself in his preface to the *New Commentary* (1984) expresses regret that *PNE* did not adopt a chronological ordering but follows instead *CP* 1933, 2nd ed. 1950. He traces again the question of editions in the 1930s, and provides some additional information that supports his own view that *PY* is the more correct text. Marcus (1987) argues for the restoration of 'Under Ben Bulben' to its rightful position at the end of *CP*, claiming that 'Politics', which is correctly placed when followed by *DC* and *P* in *Last Poems and Two Plays* (1939), is inappropriate to mark the end of Yeats' work as a poet. Needless to say, the coda has still to be written, but in the meantime, if they so wish, students can follow through this increasingly *ad hominem* argument by reading Finneran's (1984) reply to his critics.

The present situation is thoroughly unsatisfactory, and my own view is that, until critics had absorbed what Finneran was proposing in (1983), *PNE* should have been postponed. There should then have been a forum, an exchange of views and an attempt to arrive at some kind of consensus. What is at stake, after all, is how Yeats is read in the classroom. Scholars can refer to the *VE*, to MSS, and to first editions, so the primary responsibility must be towards readers, students and teachers of Yeats. On the issue of a chronological ordering, I would agree with Jeffares in his belief that this provides a more effective picture of Yeats' development as a poet, and on the issue of the order of *LP* (*PNE*) I would agree with Finneran. Ultimately, a new edition is desirable, and this should include clear indications of the different routes that have been taken towards establishing texts in which Yeats can be read with confidence.

The Reception of Yeats' Verse

An early trilogy

Of necessity my own remarks must be brief and selective, but for fuller surveys of the reception of Yeats' verse the reader is referred to Hall and Steinmann (1950), Unterecker (1963), Stallworthy (1968), Pritchard (1972), Jeffares (1977), and Cullingford (1984), though a cautionary note about these collections is perhaps in order. Although published in 1950, Hall and Steinmann contains seven essays from the 1930s, and five essays from *The Southern Review* of 1942; its bibliography, while excellent for giving a sense of the 'emergence' of Yeats in journals in the 1930s and 1940s, is therefore restricted; moreover, the title *The Permanence of Yeats* is slightly misleading, and might more properly be called 'The Reception of Yeats in the Anglo-American Academy in the 1930s and 1940s'. Pritchard's is a Leavisite reading of Yeats and the critics he admires are those who stress the human experience in Yeats – the line roughly from Leavis and L.C. Knights to C.K. Stead. Stallworthy's tidy anthology now needs revising in the light of the Finneran debate. The last essay in Cullingford dates from 1974, her justification presumably being that since 1970 'valuable critical studies of the mature poetry have been few'. Her remarks therefore are confined for the most part to a debate that belongs to the 1950s and 1960s.

Here I touch on three areas that have figured prominently in Yeats criticism and that still continue to provoke questions among students: the issue of Yeats and Symbolism, Yeats' lineage, and the relationship between his beliefs and his poetry. The intention is to provide a framework for further inquiry, to show connections, to trace outlines, and to shed light on the historical evolution of Yeats criticism. A word of caution: the issue of Yeats and the occult is glanced at here but must wait until ch. 4 for a fuller discussion; my remarks on Yeats' lineage concentrate for the most part on the Romantic inheritance – his relationship with his Irish background or with a philosophical predecessor such as Nietzsche is examined in later chapters; other areas, such as Yeats and women, Yeats and the visual arts, Yeats and language, are referred to in the final chapter. Here I take for my starting-point three essays written in the 1930s which identified particular ways of looking at Yeats and to which we can usefully return in setting down markers as to his reception.

A retrospective quality is inscribed in Yeats' work. He has the 'backward look' characteristic, as Frank O'Connor (1967) might see it, of Anglo-Irish literature as a whole. A generation after its cause had been dropped by a previous spokesperson Standish James O'Grady (1894a and 1898), he asserts the claims of Anglo-Ireland even as the latter's moment has passed. As Kenner (1987) provocatively suggests, he died, it could be said, three times – once in 1908-9 with the publication of *Collected Works*, once in 1928 with *T*, his 'grand finale', and finally in 1938-9 with 'Under Ben Bulben', where he writes his own epitaph. Yeats, it appears, flirted with death: once, in the role of postulant trying out a new ritual for his London temple, the Stella Matutina, he even lay in a coffin and listened to the ringing of 36 bells (see Howe, 1972). But, needless to say, Yeats is beguiling, and he deceived some critics into prematurely announcing his literary death. When *WSC* was published by Macmillan in 1919, Middleton Murry proclaimed Yeats' talents to be at an end and that this volume, with its lack of creative vigour, its languor and ineffectuality, its idle dreaming, marked 'Mr Yeats' Swan Song' (Jeffares, 1977). Yeats of course was partly responsible for contributing to such a reception, not least in the constant publications of 'retrospective' volumes and collections of his work. 'Hammer your thoughts into unity' has become a touchstone by which he has been assessed, but each volume seems to mark a new beginning as much as a recapitulation of the past. So criticism, always tempted historically to foreclose the discussion but invariably caught unawares, took and still takes a long time to absorb the pattern of Yeats' work. For

Yeats is the last Romantic who became a leading modern poet, the modern poet who sits uncomfortably in the modernist triumvirate of Yeats-Eliot-Pound, the Anglo-Irish 'hyphenated' poet who has been associated by some critics with Georgian Ireland (see Torchiana, 1966) and by others with the struggle against British imperialism (see Said, 1988).

Early key responses to Yeats' verse can be found in Wilson (1931), Leavis (1932) and Blackmur (1936) and we can use these to map out the subsequent critical terrain. Wilson depicts the literary history of our time as a battle between Symbolism and Naturalism, twin movements which emerged in the 19th century against the background of Romanticism and a mechanistic science. *Symbolisme* began in France and was characterised by its indefiniteness, its stress on supra-rational sensations and its attempt to communicate unique personal feelings. But the battle was never properly fought out in England, and it was left to Pater to supply Yeats with an English equivalent to French Symbolist theory. Wilson notices Yeats' maturing style and the modern poet's need of a special personality as well as an antagonism between poet and world. He places his drama with the Symbolist plays of Strindberg and Maeterlinck and shows how, in his dealings with the occult, there is always a margin of scientific doubt. Today, Wilson's reading, which it must be admitted is not in Yeats' case altogether clear, commands less assent: Yeats' symbolism in the 1890s, for example, owes as much to Irish folklore and ceremonial magic as to Pater and France. Wilson's influence, however, has been important not least in fuelling an interest in the question of Yeats, symbols and Symbolism as well as in the wider topic of Yeats and Romanticism.

Leavis stresses the debilitating influence of the Victorian poetic tradition which 'admits implicitly that the actual world is alien, recalcitrant, and unpoetical, and that no protest is worth making except the protest of withdrawal'. The trajectory of Yeats' career is from dreams to reality, an inner struggle of the 19th-century mind in an heroic form. The change between *WR* and *GH* shows the poet coming alive to the actual waking world – hard, practical, and full of modern speech – while *T* exhibits a 'ripeness in disillusion', a 'difficult and delicate sincerity'. This view of Yeats – and it should not be forgotten that Leavis, too, is a Thirties critic – has been very influential, but has become increasingly less so as more sophisticated accounts of Yeats' lineage and poetic development have been advanced. The relationship between dreaming and reality, for example, needs much more careful handling in the context of a poet who prefaced a volume entitled *Responsibilities* with the words 'in dreams begin responsibility', and who later wrote of the 'desolation of reality' that has accompanied the spread of human knowledge and civilisation.

Blackmur's essay (1936), examines the way Yeats grasped reality through magic and how this affects his stature as a poet. As a tool for poetry, magic has two major defects: firstly, no available edifice of reason can be established on it independent of its inspiration; secondly, magic promises what it cannot perform – at least in poetry, for the revelation has still to be awaited. Blackmur asks if the magical material is incorporated because of its organic reference or if its presence is merely rhetorical, and concludes that magic may be a feature of the rational imagination. Even though it does not take cognisance of Yeats' dialectical nature, his essay contains some close observation of the relationship between Yeats' poetry and his ideas.

Yeats and symbolism

The association of Yeats with French Symbolism was given its initial impetus when his friend Arthur Symons dedicated to him *The Symbolist Movement in Literature* (1899), Yeats being 'the chief representative of that movement in our country'. It was then resited, as we have seen, by Wilson within a broader context of Symbolism versus Naturalism. This was followed by Bowra (1943), who claimed that 'Yeats' career is an instructive commentary on Symbolist doctrine', and by Tindall (1945), who added a cautionary note suggesting that Yeats was a symbolist poet long before he encountered French Symbolism. These early discussions lacked sophistication regarding the concept of influence, and did not address more basic questions: for instance, if Yeats was influenced by something he must have already been open to influence, indeed, perhaps, merely seeking confirmation for ideas which were already in the process of formation. Equally, these critics were too ready to box Yeats into one particular corner, not allowing for the fact that Yeats has many contexts – not least himself. The real difficulty – leaving aside the devaluing of Yeats' autonomy as a thinker or of England's culture vis-à-vis France –

stems from uncertainty about Symbolism and how it is interpreted. According to Bowra, Yeats, unlike Mallarmé, made use of two kinds of symbols, emotional and intellectual, one connected with sounds and their association, the other with ideas. Bowra also claims that Yeats' mysticism is not 'aesthetic rapture' or 'creative ecstasy, but a belief in the powers behind the visible world'. But how we identify or assess such distinctions or claims depends on much more than a discussion about Symbolism. Grossman (1969), for example, accepts the distinction between emotional and intellectual symbols, but this is interpreted within the context of the Wisdom tradition, the Muse of Ireland, and the struggle for personal liberation, terms far removed from French Symbolism. Equally, with regard to mysticism, as the final stanza of 'Among School Children' reminds us, there is a rhapsodic quality to Yeats' work which is more than 'a belief in the powers behind the visible world'.

Before a theory of Yeats and Symbolism can be advanced, prior issues have to be resolved. We need to clarify key terms such as 'symbol', 'symbolic', 'image', 'myth', 'allegory', and distinguish between the 'incarnation' or 'transfiguration' of an image or symbol. The topic is clearly more extensive than its early formulators envisaged. A valuable survey of Yeats and symbols can be found in Seward's little-known study (1960). Seward traces the development of the symbol of the rose in western literature from ancient myths through Dante and the Catholic Middle Ages, through the Renaissance, the Romantic heritage, and onto the 20th century, where it rivals, she claims, *The Waste Land* as the symbol of our era. At each point the meaning and function of the symbol has both changed and expanded, but nothing is entirely lost; the symbol accrues meaning through time. In Medieval rhetoric, where four levels of meaning – literal, allegorical, moral and anagogical – were distinguished, the literal meaning of the rose was equated with the image of Paradise and the allegorical one with Christ's mission to humanity. Such a schema and such a view resurfaces in Yeats' multilayered symbol of the secret rose. The Romantic heritage with its new subjectivity and, later, its interest in the occult, added its own stamp, so that the rose became the focus of unorthodox transcendental longings. Later in the 19th century it was assigned a central place in Rosicrucianism. Again, both developments are there in Yeats' symbol. All this is by way of an introduction to Seward's principal concern, which is an examination of the symbol of the rose in the work of Yeats, Eliot, and Joyce (whom she unfortunately describes as 'British writers'). She pictures Yeats as the transitional figure and the first to build a new symbolic art on the ruins of Romantic hypersubjectivity. Unlike earlier critics, Seward is less dogmatic in her approach to Yeats' lineage: she shows, for example, how the volume 'The Rose' is rooted in the English tradition, how *WR* is influenced by French Symbolism, and how after 1903 Yeats left behind the symbol of the rose. Her discussion on Eliot and tradition, and on Joyce and his synthesis of modern, romantic, and medieval sources, is often illuminating, but she devotes too little attention to the possible interconnections. When Joyce, for example, begins *A Portrait of the Artist as a Young Man* (1916) by referring to the 'wild rose blossoms/On the little green place', he reminds us not only how the symbol of the rose can be given a political inflection, but also how it builds on the work of Yeats' secret rose, whose hour, as we are told in the preface to *SR*, has surely come.

The connection between Yeats and Symbolism has prompted several different kinds of inquiry. Seward's study delineates a broader context than is to be found in, say, Wilson; she believes that for a proper understanding of Yeats' symbols a much longer history needs to be invoked. Another approach, well represented by Stauffer (1949), has fastened onto the changing use of symbols within Yeats' work as a whole. Symbols in Yeats' verse – Stauffer's principal examples are the gyre and the swan – are 'always getting tangled...with other symbols'; they are better understood if we know the way they are deployed elsewhere. According to Stauffer, Yeats is 'incorrigibly a lyric poet whose imagination is set in vivid symbolic visual patterns'. In passing, it can be noted that Stauffer's emphasis on the relatedness of Yeats' symbols anticipates both Kenner's essay (1955) and the more complex argument of Engelberg (1964), while his stress on Yeats' lyricism is countered by Parkinson's view that Yeats is primarily a dramatic poet.

The influence of the occult on Yeats' symbols is another important topic, and while the occult as such is treated in ch. 4 it needs some commentary here. Yeats' essay on magic (*E & I*), where he states that the 'great memory can be evoked by symbols', reminds us of the close association between his poetry and the occult. His interest in the occult precedes any possible influence by French Symbolism and casts an aura round his symbols that can be fully explained only by reference to his involvement in ceremonial magic. When in 1890 AE joined the Theosophical Society and Yeats the Order of the Golden Dawn, they parted ways because AE's interests lay with mysticism and seeing the astral light, while Yeats desired a more tangible communication with the spirits. Later, what distinguished Yeats from other members of the Order was his wish not so much to follow a Rosicrucian/Christian way of spirituality but to study magic and theurgy (Raine, 1986). Symbols in Yeats' early verse come clothed in the garments of ceremonial magic, with the poet as mage and adept, summoning up the spirits inside or beyond the universe. Even though he became disillusioned with the Golden Dawn after the ugly confrontation between Mathers and the London Temple in 1900 (see Harper, 1974), and even though he increasingly sided with Art against the Adept (see O'Donnell, 1976), the presence of magic underlies Yeats' use of symbols, so that when he writes out in a verse the names of the leaders of the Easter Rising he is, as Young (1975) well observes, like the mage effecting what he does in words.

The issue of Yeats and symbolism is set fair to continue. Donoghue (1971) roots the discussion within an argument about power, how magic and poetry are forms of power, how Yeats is concerned with making a masterful style, how moral questions are answered in aesthetic terms, how Nietzsche, therefore, is the crucial figure intervening between Blake and Yeats. Symbolism is the literary form of magic, the difference being that what the mage does consciously the poet does 'half consciously and half by instinct'. But against the symbol stands history, and in an insightful chapter, 'History and the Secret Discipline', Donoghue shows how this opposition of symbol and history produced in Yeats not the single response but an awareness of tension between the two. Thus, while *WSC* stresses an accommodation with history, where history is consistent with symbolism, *T* is symbolism 'glancing ruefully at history'. History and symbol, truth and system, are like rival allegiances, and fortunately, according to Donoghue, Yeats has a weakness for reality. In his best poems, therefore, we see him mastering but not resolving conflict.

Yeats' lineage

One effect of Wilson's study was to direct attention to the poet's literary and cultural heritage. In a sense, of course, Yeats had given one important clue to his position on the literary map when in 1893, with Edwin Ellis, he edited a book on Blake and when in 1937 in 'The Municipal Gallery Revisited' he referred to himself as one of the 'last Romantics'. Yeats and Romanticism, a topic well suited for revealing how Yeats has been received by his critics, has been approached from several different angles. Two important formative studies assessing the links between Yeats and Blake were undertaken in the 1950s by Rudd (1953) and Adams (1955). The essential difference between Blake and Yeats discerned by Rudd is that while the former is a prophet, the latter is simply an 'enchanter'. In Blake the world is transfigured through the eyes of love; he defies dualism by postulating an incarnate God who overcomes the false god, Urizen. Yeats, on the other hand, is content to cast a spell over the reader. Moreover, having no supernatural vision, and being primarily interested in himself and in the division in himself, Yeats 'substituted vacillation for belief'. This narrowly focused inquiry is forcefully argued, but it does less than justice to Yeats. The clarity of Blake's voice belongs to the Romantic age, and if Yeats' rings less clear this stems in part from his living in a period of late Romanticism, when perceptions of the nature of reality as well as of the relationship between art and reality had dramatically altered. A marked characteristic of this period is its introspective and often frenetic attempts to realign the present with the past. Equally, Yeats' interest in ceremonial magic deserves more than the cavalier treatment to be found in Rudd, who claims that most of it 'cannot be taken seriously'. In fact, this is precisely what later critics have done – though this is not to say they endorse any of it.

Adams' aim is to compare the two poets in their use of symbolism; he is not primarily concerned with the question of influence, but rather with how the two poets looked at the same world from different perspectives. He outlines Blake's aesthetic in terms of its epistemology, its true vision (which he identifies as a vision of apocalypse, or total resolution where the unity of reality is revealed), and its debased vision (or moral allegorisation). In Blake the single image draws into it all the minute particulars, where what seemed contraries are shown to be equally true.

Throughout this informative discussion of Blake, Adams brings out how Yeats is like a common man caught in a fallen world, and how, in contrast with Blake, his poetry enacts the difficulty of achieving the vision we find in Blake. In Yeats' early poetry the subject-object dichotomy is unsolved; later, he begins to champion Blakean action, but he never transcends the problem of duality, not even in *AV* where the single geometrical conception is composed of two symbols, one superimposed on the other, namely the Great Wheel and the interlocking cones. Adams' version of Yeats reveals a poet conscious of limits, aware that he is not a mystic, who shares the same world as Blake but approaches it from a different angle. For Adams, this enhances rather than detracts from Yeats' stature as a poet, and the Byzantium poems, for example, are 'truly great poems for the reason that they dramatise their own failure as truly visionary documents'.

Traces of Adams' argument, as when he writes that Yeats 'could not bring himself to share his predecessor's faith in a world transformed by a vision of love and beauty', can be found in Bornstein (1970). Here, though, the comparison is between Yeats and Shelley. This study contrasts the intellectual vision of early Yeats with the antinomial vision of his later period, with 1903 as the dividing year. The early Yeats, in his search for intellectual beauty, follows Shelley in both theme and imagery, but instead of the star and the cosmopolitan settings Yeats substituted the Rose and Ireland. Until 1900 Yeats denied Shelley's influence, and, moreover, sought to identify the origins of his predecessor's symbols in the ancient world. After 1903 the antinomial vision, with its 'movement downwards upon life, not upwards out of life' (*L*, p. 469), began to emerge. The material present now rivalled the ideal, joy replaced sorrow, and the grey of Ireland overcame the colours of Shelley's Italy. In an interesting chapter where he juxtaposes Shelley's epipsyche and Yeats' Doctrine of the Mask, Bornstein shows how the mature Yeats wrestled wih Shelley's idea of love and how he eventually replaced *pax amoris* with *bellum amoris*. A chapter on their views of history, embodied by Athens and Byzantium, contrasts Shelley's elevation of an actual historical period (490-322 BC) with Yeats' Byzantium, which exists as an ideal in opposition to the natural world of generation. In a final chapter Bornstein defends Shelley from Yeats' charge that he lacked a Vision of Evil, and stresses how they differ not so much on this as on the presentation of evil in art. For Shelley, art should inspire and show the triumph of justice; for the mature Yeats, reality and justice go hand in hand. In a subsequent inquiry looking at modernism in terms of acts of mind, Bornstein (1976) reflects again on the last Romanticism of Yeats, this time in the context of Eliot and Stevens. Making use of the idea of the 'Greater Romantic Lyric', he asks whether Yeats' art deserves to be seen as a continuation of Romantic tradition; his conclusion is that many of the greatest mature poems written between 1918 and 1929 'creatively develop out of romantic themes and modes'.

Such studies remind us of some of the issues involved in tracing Yeats' lineage, but they tend to avoid making distinctions between influence and pattern, an acknowledged debt and a rejected influence. Moreover, they do not tackle more difficult theoretical issues concerned with Yeats' unconscious, whether he merely found confirmation for his own ideas in his predecessors, or, given that Yeats is one of the 'last Romantics', how the relationship between early and late Romanticism is to be described. Bloom (1970), on the other hand, in a challenging study of Yeats' place in the English poetic tradition, confronts such questions. With Freud in mind, Bloom tells us 'poetic influence...is a variety of melancholy or an anxiety-principle'. In coming to terms with his predecessors Yeats is involved in a complicated revisionary reading, and in his swerves away from them – 'clinamen' is the term Bloom uses – he reveals the nature of his debt and influence.

Bloom traces a line from Shelley through Browning and Pater to Yeats. Yeats' typical poem is a dramatic lyric that behaves as if it were a fragment of a mythological romance where the poet as quest-hero undertakes an odyssey of spirit. The internalised quest-romance is the structure uniting Shelley's Alastor with *WO* and *SW*. Browning's antithetical quest, on the other hand, which ended with the permanent suffering of the self alone, was a warning to Yeats. Pater bequeathed to Yeats an impossible aesthetic ideal, a desperate trust in the flux of experience and an acknowledged rift between consciousness and experience. The 'Tragic Generation' of Dowson and Johnson, Yeats' immediate predecessors, were also warnings, for they lacked the human strength to put their faith in art alone. These are the strands Bloom isolates in Yeats' lineage. Specific chapters on Shelley and Blake underline Yeats' conflicting attitudes towards the former and his swerves away from the latter. Juxtaposing Blake and Yeats shows Yeats to be a Gnostic, a dualist, longing for a future after death, exalting the Shadow, caught in his early career in a solipsistic reverie. Blake, on the other hand, whom Yeats wrongly imagines is a Pre-Raphaelite, insists that the emotional and the natural, fused in 'the condition of fire', form a single reality. Bloom's persuasive commentary in ch. 14 on *AV* reinforces this difference between the two. For Blake and Gnosticism, the Creation and the Fall are one event and daimons have to be exorcised; the Shadow, though a selfhood, is a stifler. For Yeats, on the other hand, the world is fallen, the Shadow is the creative self, and daimons, especially the anti-self, need to be embraced.

In the actual survey of Yeats' work, Bloom seems to lose sight of the issue of influence and concentrates on a series of critical discriminations about the particular merits of individual poems or books. The early poetry of 1885-99 he values higher than the middle poems of 1899-1914; *PASL* (1918), a 'masterpiece in the tradition of marmoreal reveries', and the product of a crucial period in Yeats' imaginative life (1915-17), is promoted above *AV*. In contrast with Rudd, Bloom admires a poem like 'Vacillation' precisely because it shows Yeats doubting his own mythologies. The most illuminating remarks occur in his discussion of the Great Wheel, his comments on 'A Second Coming', and his promotion of the early poetry and *PASL*. How much we need Bloom's Freudian anxiety-of-influence concept is an open question, but setting Yeats against the background of Blake and the Romantic inheritance highlights at once the continuity of a tradition and its decline, and raises doubts, as Bloom rightly observes, about Yeats' modern humanistic vision and its representative status or otherwise.

Other studies, such as Hough (1947), Kermode (1957) and Fletcher (1987), have focused on the late 19th-century context. Hough examines the genesis of Yeats' ideas in English aestheticism. With Ruskin, Rossetti, Morris, Pater, and the aesthetes behind him, Yeats cuts a different figure from when he is cast against a Romantic background. For Hough, Yeats takes his colouring from Victorian culture, from the opposition of art and society; by 1850 the strong ethical and social bias had spawned its antithesis, its opposition in art, and by 1870 there was an

Aesthetic Movement. Stressing the significance of the visual world, Ruskin pleaded for the integration of visual sensibility with the rest of psychic life, of art with religious experience. Both he and Morris attempted to make the world fit for artists to live in. Rossetti, claims Hough, inaugurated a period of emotional unrest. A conscious aesthete, he sought satisfaction in traditional religious symbolism but was possessed of a love that could never be satisfied, and it was this impasse and the movement inwards to the self that provided Yeats' starting-point. In contrast with Arnold's search for certainty, Pater emphasised the flux of experience. Feeling and sincerity acted as touchstones for an assessment of life, and he sought, therefore, a world outside of turbulence, a home to which he could withdraw. In his discussion of the *fin-de-siècle*, Hough repeats the view that Yeats learnt of French Symbolism through Symons and stresses that Axel became for a time the poet's sacred book. Unlike the other Rhymers, however, Yeats had the tenacity and spiritual energy to take the aesthetic project further. Hough shows by implication how Yeats questions all his predecessors. Rossetti confused the physical and the spiritual; Morris sought a new mythology in romantic medievalism, but for Yeats poetry needed to recover contact with religion, the people and history. Unlike Morris, whose poetry was divorced from its age, Yeats draws more from contemporary Ireland than from Celtic legend and he directly engages with the life of his times. Hough concludes his study with a chapter on Yeats, but he might have reflected more explicitly on the poet's links with the specified tradition. It is not altogether clear, for example, how his discussion of the occult relates to his overall thesis about the last Romantics, or how much weight is to be attached to Yeats' Irish context, or whether Yeats, especially in the light of his (modernist) rejection of rhetoric, is a Victorian or a modern thinker and poet.

Yeats is both central and tangential to Kermode's study. Thus, much of the discussion in Part One is devoted to Yeats; on the other hand, Yeats seems to be there to illustrate a separate argument about the Romantic basis of modern literature. Kermode links the isolation of the artist – the Romantic theme – with the modern predeliction for the Image, and he finds in Yeats the exemplary figure. The alienation of the artist from society deepened in the 19th century and found new articulation in the work of Arnold and Pater. Kermode stresses this native English tradition in contrast with French Symbolism, which he reads as a later version of Romanticism. His initial discussion of Yeats concentrates on 'In Memory of Major Robert Gregory', an elegy that expresses the predicament of the artist or contemplative in a world built for action. Yeats, in love with action, is held back from full engagement by his own artistic temperament and by the age in which he lives: hence his admiration for an artist like Gregory who has escaped into action, but who becomes in the process an image of the artist who did not escape. At the same time Yeats also discovered in the Dancer the great image that reconciled action and contemplation, and in the Tree the contrasting integrity of the Image which stood outside time and science and which could not therefore be subjected to any (Eliotic or Symbolist) form of dissociation. In this sense Yeats, fully conscious of his heritage, worked through both the nature of the poet's isolation and the problem of the Image. Part Two is devoted to exposing the Romantic roots of modernist critical theory. Kermode outlines Hulme's influence which bequeathed to the English tradition a 'modernised, but essentially traditional, aesthetic of Symbolism'; he comments on the way the Vortex overcomes the stillness in the Image, takes issue with the Symbolist 'dissociation of sensibility', and contrasts Yeats and Eliot in their understanding of the relationship between Image and life. At each point Yeats is held up as the central figure, the isolated artist who sought to overcome his isolation by Unity of Being as expressed in the Image.

Though often recommended, the overall value of Kermode's book for students of Yeats remains uncertain. There is something external in his discussion of Yeats, a remoteness that comes from seeing him too readily as an exemplary figure. Kermode emphasises the Romantic Image selectively, and aspects of the Image that do not fit his argument are omitted. If the idea of the isolation of the artist were really put to work in the case of Yeats, it would need serious qualification – think of his roles in the public domain as co-Director of the Abbey, the founder of a literary movement, an active Senator; or think of 'The Municipal Gallery Revisited' and his wish to be remembered because he 'had such friends'. As regards the Image, this again, especially in the light of the studies on symbolism referred to above, is too abstract a concept for an inquiry into Yeats' work, and again requires closer definition. It is worth referring to the organicist tradition of metaphor that underlies Yeats' use of the Image, but only if we notice how he departs from such a tradition. The natural world in Yeats looks very different from its depiction in Romantic verse: it is never a subject in its own right, rarely challenges, does not share the same life-force as the human world, and its symbolic quality often insists on itself throughout. We might add that the natural world is often relegated to a term in a structured, dialectical argument, and looks not unlike part of the first stage in the adept's ascent to spiritual knowledge. As de Man (1984) rightly notices, Yeats' emblematic landscape differs fundamentally from Wordsworth's transcendental vision. Moreover, between the image and the emblem there is a conflict, an ambiguity, an area of discontinuity which Yeats sought to bridge but could not. Against Kermode's trumpeting of the 'reconciliatory image' in 'Among School Children', de Man suggests that the final line is an anguished question: 'to choose the dancer means to fall into the transient world of matter for the sake of a few moments of illusive pleasure; to choose the dance means to renounce all natural joys for the sake of divine revelation'. Yeats, therefore, affords no reassurance from the 'anxieties of our post-romantic predicament'.

Avoiding the problems that beset the single-stranded thesis, Fletcher combines biography with research, and in an informative series of essays on late 19th-century figures associated with Yeats he fills in gaps in our knowledge of his lineage. His essay outlining the English Aesthetic Movement, though not directly relevant to Yeats, is suggestive, mirroring as it does the course of the painter's son from art student to writer. His 1957 essay on Bedford Park contextualises the four years Yeats spent in London, 1887-91, surrounded by a self-conscious artistic community that took to dressing up and performing plays. Other essays on Althea Gyles, the Gore-Booth sisters, Johnson, Gray and Arthur Symons, strengthen our understanding of the biographical context to Yeats' work. This is supplemented by Fletcher's parallel interest in *A*, where he is concerned not so much with identifying figures mentioned in the text as with the larger patterns and rhythms that Yeats sought to embrace in his quest for 'self-transparency'. In *R*, whose title signifies not an escape into the past but 'an attempt to distinguish pattern', Yeats places himself in history, and finds rhythm in history. Fletcher also reminds us of the varied nature of this discovery of pattern. Thus, *R* was composed in the shadow of the seven years prior to 1914; Yeats' attempt to situate himself in history conflicted with his 'responsibilities' to the present; he needed to discover rhythm in the self before it could be recognised in history; he learnt from Pater that memory operates discontinuously; *R* is 'surprisingly devoid of social context'. He might well have gone on to contrast Gosse's autobiography (1907) with *R*, or Le Gallienne's (1926) atmospheric picture of 'wonderful London' with Yeats' retrospective account of 'The Tragic Generation' in *A* (also first published in 1926), for it is in such kinds of detailed inquiries that Fletcher's work has distinguished itself.

Yeats' poetry and his beliefs

Yeats' beliefs have often been dismissed by critics as silly or out-of-keeping with a scientific age, though in recent years there has been a tendency to cast them in a more positive light. Part of the problem is that we are still living with the 1930s legacy and are still uncertain how to deal dispassionately with Yeats' occult ideas. Blackmur's essay (1936), for example, still reads well today, but it bears the scars of the Hard Fact Thirties when critics felt obliged to separate Yeats' poetry from his convictions. In this section, with particular reference to Auden (1939), MacNeice (1941), Spender (1935), Muir (1940), Daiches (1940), Brooks (1939), Tate (1942), Ellmann (1954) and Winters (1960), I retrace the contours of that critical terrain, conscious always that it was not Yeats' personality that posed a problem for critics of the 1930s and 1940s, as Cullingford (1984) maintains, but his 'System' of beliefs.

Critics differ in the value they attach to Yeats' System. Rajan (1965) is not untypical in following Yeats' suggestion that *AV* gave the poet 'metaphors for poetry'. Yeats' vision is thus best approached as 'a group of interrelated symbols', and, because it is a myth or a framework, it should be imaginatively rather than literally received. As regards the importance of the System for an interpretation of the poetry, Rajan asserts that 'it is to the poetry that we should direct ourselves, and though esoteric interpretation is sometimes helpful and at other times necessary, it has to be controlled by a firm sense of the poem'. Malins (1974) goes further, claiming that *AV* is 'vital to a full understanding of how his poetry was nourished'. Some critics have noticed how Yeats' great poetry after 1917 coincides with the development of his

System, the composition of which can be traced from *PASL* (1918), through the period of automatic writing from October 1917 to March 1920, to its final shape in *AV* (1925-6). Other critics, however, choose to distinguish the poetry from the System or, more generally, from his ideas.

Kermode (1967) observes that Yeats' true commitment was not to the System but to poetry. The System, however, enabled him to see justice and reality together, to understand, that is, the tension between eternity and the dying generations. He laboured to speak in terms of a modern reality without forfeiting the use of paradigms, so that 'the whole history of Yeats' style...reflects this regard for the reality that will not be reduced'. As a poet, the dream never wholly enchanted Yeats, but as a thinker, unfortunately, it did. His poetry is therefore the product of a sceptical gaze, but in his thinking he gravitates towards authoritarian politics and the dream (or 'fiction' in Kermode's terms) of apocalypse and crisis. Hassett (1986), in a recent, original inquiry into the place of hatred in the poet's life and thought, suggests that, though often motivated by hatred, Yeats managed to control it when writing verse. At the end of his forthright essay condemning Yeats' fascist tendencies, O'Brien (1965) has the awkward task of returning to the connection between poetry and politics. He negotiates the dilemma not in the more conventional terms of admiring the poetry and hating the politics, but, instead, by trying to account for the force which surfaces in both the political prose and the poetry. O'Brien develops this by suggesting that Yeats' poetry anticipates Hitler and the Second World War but in 'metaphors of such power that they thrust aside all calculated intent'. O'Brien's argument, which is examined in more detail in ch. 5 below, is particularly strained at this point, and serves to illustrate yet again the continuing difficulty critics encounter in incorporating Yeats' beliefs, whether religious or political, into a reading of his poetry.

When Yeats died in January 1939, the 1930s era was already being confined to history, its fate sealed for a generation or more by the condemnation of Leavis (1940), Orwell (1940), Auden, and others. Leavis called it 'the Marxist decade', Auden in 'September 1st 1939' 'a low dishonest decade', while Orwell thought that 'the literary history of the thirties seems to justify the opinion that a writer does well to keep out of politics'. Yeats seemed out of time and place, and this worked both for and against him. Because he was not associated with what some considered the cul- de-sac of the 1930s, his reputation was enhanced. He was for Eliot 'a great and permanent example...of what I have called Character of the Artist' (1940). Equally, because of his stature and because he was inimitable, younger writers such as Auden, Spender and MacNeice could admire him with a certain detachment and without envy. But on the debit side there were his reactionary politics and his heterodox mysticism, and it is this accusatory view of Yeats that the 1930s bequeathed to posterity. Today, we are more inclined to see Yeats as one of the Moderns rather than as the poet who survived and who cannot be easily categorised.

'You were silly like us: your gift survived it all', wrote Auden in March 1939 in his famous elegy (1939a), the gift being 'language' and the ability to write well. Such an opposition is erected into a court-room drama when Auden (1939) presents in turn the case for the prosecution and the defence. In Thirties style, the prosecution points to three accusations the public might have against Yeats: (i) that he does not have a gift for memorable language, (ii) that he did not have a profound understanding of the age he lived in, and (iii) that he was unsympathetic towards the advanced thought of his time. Formulated thus, they of course miss the mark. 'How many of his lines can you remember?' asks the Prosecutor rather foolishly about a poet who is famous for his aphorisms and his quotable lines. The second and third accusations now seem dated, and are turned on their head by the Defence. Yeats' convictions can be better understood in the wider context of the failure of liberal capitalist democracy, and the rise of Irish nationalism. Against the atomisation of the individual under capitalism, Yeats sought 'a binding force of society'; it was a religious search, and the religious solution may be unworkable, but to Yeats' credit it was based on a 'true perception of a social evil'. In conclusion, the Defence reminds the court that Yeats was a poet and not a politician, that art is the product of history, not a cause, and that his diction shows a steady evolution towards 'the true democratic style'. Although probably unintended, Auden's essay and elegy, with their no-nonsense rationality, hardnosed realism and superior air, have widened the gap between Yeats' poetry and what he believed, and as a result it has proved difficult either to avoid the obligation to defend him, or to reshape the relationship between his occult ideas and his verse.

MacNeice (1941), in what for Ellmann is 'still as good an introduction to [Yeats] as we have', conducts an extended debate with both High Modernism and the 1930s. As he proclaims in his preface, 'a poem is both about something but [it] also *is*'. Doubtless with Auden in mind, he seeks to rebut those who maintain that 'Yeats was a silly old thing but he was a *poet*'. There is an intimate connection, he posits in ch. 1, between a poem, the author's life and a wider society; and the value of poetry resides in its truthfulness to life. In his concluding chapter – and it is a view supported by the study as a whole – MacNeice suggests that, in spite of thriving on theoretical half-truths, preaching an unsound doctrine on poetry, or promulgating distortions about his family, mysticism and Ireland, 'Yeats, as a poet, is characterised by integrity'. Some of his guiding principles may have been wrong, but there is no guarantee that with the right beliefs he would have written better poetry. Indeed, MacNeice adds, he may not have written at all if he had thought differently. It is to Yeats' credit that he went against the age, and if he is to be an example it is that we should write according to our lights. In taking issue with the vulgar Marxism of the time, which saw poetry as wholly determined by an economic base, or in his passing references to *Goodbye Twilight*, a collection of proletarian poems now almost entirely forgotten, MacNeice reveals his Thirties colours. But through it all, a picture of Yeats emerges that commands respect. Unlike his contemporary AE, MacNeice maintains, Yeats was not a mystic; he was fascinated by the metaphysical dialectic of Being and Becoming; he mistakenly thought he could approach popular poetry via an esoteric world; he recognised that a poem – a bridge to the Unknown – had to be constructed in terms of the known; and he learnt to compromise with the language of men, eventually adopting an admirably hard and dry style. As to what he believed, 'there was always a sceptic in Yeats'. MacNeice stresses Yeats' Irish background and his connections with other Irish writers, how he fused Symbolist with nationalist doctrine, and how nationalism crucially intervened in saving him from theosophy and 1890s aestheticism. And politically, MacNeice argues, citing Auden's speech for the Defence, he should not be dismissed as 'a mere reactionary'. One of the strengths of MacNeice's study is to demonstrate that Yeats was both in and out of touch with his age: he shared much with other modern writers such as Rilke, Eliot,

Lawrence, or other Irish writers such as Joyce, AE or Synge, but he was also his own man, who, for all his campaigning, in the end refused discipleship.

Spender (1935), Muir (1939) and Daiches (1940) add other Thirties voices to the debate, this time in the wider context of modern literature and poetry. Spender, whose criticism is rooted in the familiar if unsophisticated opposition between romanticism and realism, attempts to detach the poetry from the beliefs. Thus, Yeats' occult activity has 'little relation to the part that the theory of magic plays in his poetry'; his theory of symbolism is 'orthodoxly psychological'; his method is most successful when applied to objects which are the least symbolic; his attitude to magical events is like a doctor's, not a witch doctor's, while his poetry is 'only magical in the sense that he can produce a certain atmosphere'. Spender, therefore, admires the poetry not for its magic or its mystery but for its 'passion, its humanity, its occasional marvellous lucidity, its technical mastery, its integrity, its strength, its reality and its opportunism'. Perhaps his most telling criticism comes in claiming that 'Yeats has found, as yet, no subject of moral significance in the social life of his time. Instead of a subject, he offers us magnificent and lively *rapportage* about his friends'. For Muir, the present is a transitional period and such periods 'encourage apocalyptic visions or the historical sense'. Unlike Kermode above, Muir is untroubled by this, content merely to have identified what he takes to be the determining historical context. This leaves him free to fasten onto different features of Yeats' work: the relevance of *AV* to an understanding of the poetry; how great poems such as 'The Second Coming', 'Leda and the Swan', and the Byzantium poems gain from a knowledge of Yeats' occult ideas; moreover, the intensity of even his occasional poems derives from the System – a point not often noticed. Taking his cue from Spender, Muir contrasts the range of Yeats' imagination with his narrow sympathies and alerts us to the way he lacks 'moral immediacy'. Daiches (1940) comes to conclusions similar to those of MacNeice. Yeats was not a mystical poet; to help him achieve an adequate poetic expression he needed a system, order and ritual; his early poetry indicates a need for pattern, which he found in folk material; Ireland rescued him from his imitative romanticism, so that by *WR* Irish themes and figures predominate. In a later review, significantly entitled 'The Practical Visionary'

(1962), Daiches continues such a line of interpretation: Yeats was not an esoteric; Ireland saved him from the Rhymers' Club; 'the test of a philosophy was the degree to which illuminating poetry could be based on it, not vice-versa'. He concludes that Yeats was a shrewd and practical person, whose life and work formed a unity.

In American criticism, the issue of Yeats' beliefs and his poetry has been coloured both by the Hard Fact Thirties and by the presence of New Criticism. At the end of his chapter on Yeats, Brooks (1939) summarises what the System gave the poet: concrete and traditional symbols, the ability to see the world as a great drama, a pattern which was flexible enough to allow for the complexity of experience and to take in the whole person, and a doctrine of the Mask which enabled him to break decisively with the optimism, decorum and sentimentality of Victorian poetry. Brooks' concern is not with the (Thirties) issue of the truth or falsity of Yeats' System, but rather with how it constitutes a world-view, the ' "utterance of the whole soul of man" having for its object imaginative contemplation'. Brooks' argument is pressed a little more sharply, if not effectively countered, in Tate (1942), who claims that Yeats is *not* a Romantic, that his System is not a mythology but an extended metaphor, that his poetry does not illustrate the System, that the doctrine of the conflict of opposites says nothing about the fundamental nature of reality but is rather a dramatic framework, and (prophetically!) that scholars in the coming generation will neglect the poetry for a study of the ideas.

Close to the centre of the New Critical view of Yeats is the issue of how much we need to know in order to appreciate the poetry. Brooks makes use of the System as expounded in *AV*, while Tate prefers to rely on 'the ordinary critical equipment of the educated critic' (1942). Ellmann (1954), alert both to his own biographical leanings and to the New Criticism, prefers an analytical approach. In his chapter 'Assertion Without Doctrine', he makes three observations. Firstly, taking up the last comment in Brooks' chapter, he submits – in a way which recalls Spender's remarks that the later poems rest on certain qualities such as 'breeding' and 'courtesy' rather than on beliefs – that for Yeats a belief is primarily a conviction. Moreover, beliefs have to be welded into a poem, which is not, therefore, merely an expression of belief; the test of an idea is not its significance outside the poem but 'its relevance to the speaker's situation'. Secondly, ideas in Yeats exist to be wrestled with and overpowered. His poetry is a site of conflict where ideas are altered or qualified according to the context of the poem. Yeats' belief in reincarnation, his view of heaven or the end of the world, his religious imagery all undergo modification in his poetry. He can be sceptical about reincarnation, startlingly variable about heaven, mixed in his attitude towards eschatology and an upholder by turns of both Eastern religion and Western thought. Ellmann concludes that the essential standard for the poet is one of 'dwelling in the presence of certain ideas', rather than of positing them as truths demanding adherence. Thirdly, in line with Symbolist theory, Ellmann affirms that the centre of a Yeats poem is not its ideological content but its mood. Moods elevate the imagination above reason; they unify the world into one imaginative substance; they can be forcefully expressed (especially important for someone with a flexible point of view); they admit the poet into areas forbidden the scientist or clergyman in possession of a more confident attachment to reality. These kinds of discrimination may not map out the whole ground for a study of Yeats' poetry and beliefs, but they certainly demonstrate the scope of what might be involved.

Hill's brief, profound and deliberately inconclusive essay (1971) – 'meditation' is a better word than essay – takes issue with Ellmann's view that Yeats 'remained stubbornly loyal to the conscious mind's intelligible structure'. Following Simone Weil's suggestion that 'the simultaneous composition on several planes' is the law of artistic creation, Hill suggests that poetry recognises the primary objective world 'not so much by exercising its discursive faculty as by enacting a paradigm'. As heir to the Romantic tradition, Yeats was involved in distinguishing true from false masks. The true mask could be shaped either as a 'grammar of assent', where there is a reciprocity between imagination and action, or as 'syntax' or 'articulate energy'. When Burke, recognising the force of the contemptible, 'returns upon himself' at the end of 'Thoughts on French affairs', or when Arnold in brooding on 'Empedocles on Etna' writes 'there is everything to be endured, nothing to be done', they illustrate what Hill means by syntax, 'the conscious mind's intelligible structure'. For a poet without a grammar of assent, there is a dichotomy: at best syntax, at worst manic or depressive phases. This is Yeats' error: 'In Yeats' poetry there is imagination; in Yeats' politics there is action; but the one does not enrich or deepen the other'. What Hill admires about Yeats' poetry is the energy of his syntax, the 'return upon himself', as in the final lines of 'The Second Coming'. Hill goes on to suggest that 'Easter 1916' is a paradigm of the hard-won sanctity of the intellect, which distinguishes it from Newman's grammar of assent, or Arnold's negative conversion, or Milosz's validity of moments of consciousness. This complex set of discriminations needs close attention and serves to remind us that the issue of Yeats' poetry and beliefs is correspondingly intricate. Hill's essay should not be overlooked either in a consideration of Yeats' politics.

Since the formative period of the late 1930s and early 1940s, some Yeats critics have assumed in dealing with the issue of Yeats' ideas and his poetry that they are first in the field or that others have simply got it wrong. Winters (1960) provides a good example; he joins the debate like someone breaking up a party. He accepts the need to take Yeats' ideas seriously, and summarises them thus: all good stems from emotions; lust and rage are paraded; ignorance is valued; an agrarian society run by a landed gentry is desirable. Yeats admired women for their beauty, had a cyclical view of history, believed in Irish legends, and praised and mythologised his friends. Winters then attacks individual poems, raising doubts, for example, about the last sestet of 'Leda and the Swan' and especially the final question, given that the rest of the poem provides no clues. The vehicle of the poem is a Greek myth but the tenor is Yeats' private myth, and to take the poem seriously we have to believe what Yeats believed; that history moves in cycles, that the rape of Leda inaugurated a new cycle, and so on. For Winters, Yeats' poems are inflated, full of medieval symbolism ('perne in a gyre'), clichéd (a 'Ledaean body'), given to verbiage ('a terrible beauty'); his obscurity is not Mallarméan, but arises from confusion of thought, ineptitude of style, and the intense privacy of his symbols.

Chapter 3
Yeats' Drama

Introductions and Texts

Eric Bentley (1954), in a comment probably still valid today, once remarked, 'It cannot be said that Yeats has much of a reputation as a playwright'. Yeats' plays are not widely performed and when they are it is to a restricted, often academic, audience. This situation has existed for a long time and it is difficult to see how it will be altered. Hogan (1968), playing the devil's advocate, summarises the case against Yeats: without superb performances his plays remain painfully dull; the later plays are private statements unsuited for the theatre; they are undramatic, static, with little interest in plot or character; finally, Yeats was never fundamentally interested in the theatre and knew little about it. Lucas (1963), in a slightly condescending belletristic way, suggests that Yeats was a poet through and through, that his true mistress was not drama but the 'Muse of Lyric', and, more damning still, that he was hampered by introversion, lack of observation and weak dramatic theory. Yeats has not been without powerful advocates, but there has been no significant breakthrough in finding new audiences, and his plays remain relatively unknown and unappreciated. It is more often than not assumed that 'Yeats' means poetry and not drama. But it is worth remembering that Bentley called Yeats a 'considerable playwright', and that Eliot declared, 'I do not know where our debt to him as a dramatist ends – and in time it will not end until that drama itself ends' (1940). The best advice is to approach the plays without prejudice, try to see a performance, and listen to what those involved in dramatising his work have to say.

The best companion study of specific plays is Jeffares and Knowland (1975), but for a general introduction Ure (1963b) can be recommended. Eschewing a chronological ordering, Ure uses mixed criteria, examining, for example, Yeats' revisions, the connection between theory and practice, the place of irony and myth, the issue of remoteness and realism and the choice of theme and image. Such an approach works well, for in this way certain exemplary routes into Yeats' drama can be explored. In his discussion of *CK*, Ure traces the four revisions to the 1892 version (1895, 1901, 1912, 1919), and notices the continuous enlargement of Aleel's role, and how the theme of the Saint versus the Artist becomes more pronounced. *CK* is an episodic play, but the revisions suggest another kind of play in the making, a single episode explored in depth. Other plays Ure groups according to genre (such as the Cuchulain or miracle plays), beasts (such as *The Unicorn from the Stars*, *The Player Queen* and *The Herne's Egg*), or life cycle from cradle to grave (such as *The Dreaming of the Bones*, *The Words upon the Window Pane*, and *Purgatory*). At each point his illuminating comments make the plays more accessible, though the book as a whole suffers from uneveness and is also somewhat dated, its discussion being largely restricted to critical works produced between 1950 and 1960. It can be supplemented by his essays on Yeats' drama (1974) where he explores the use of poetry and prose in the plays, the pivotal position of *GH* as the first play in which Yeats abandoned blank verse for the rhyming 'heroic fourteener', and how this led eventually to the three- and four-stress syllabic line of *P*. Yeats' early plays, such as *CK*, *The Player Queen*, and *Deirdre*, reveal the history of the great poet's mind and the position of the poet in modern society. They enabled him, according to Ure, to maintain his integrity, his ideal of an imaginative coherence between poet and audience.

Taylor (1984) provides another helpful guide. He underlines the ritual quality in the plays, their stylisation, magic and their connection with *AV*. He discusses Yeats' concept of tragedy, how at the heart of this is the question of orthodox form and interpretation, how Yeats stressed the passionate moment of personal crisis, and how, to attain heroic stature, the individual must consciously interact with his/her anti-self. In his summaries of each play, Taylor draws attention to themes and language, dwells on the importance of *SW*, discounts the autobiographical elements in *The Only Jealousy of Emer*, and concludes by emphasising not so much the esoteric as the dramatic qualities of the plays. He also notices the shift from the idealised spiritual existence of the early plays to the celebration of passion in the later ones, and comments on Yeats' technical development as a playwright.

Yeats' plays have proved textually less controversial than his verse. *CPl* is based on the 1934 edition, which was reissued in 1952 with the addition of *A Full Moon in March*, *The King of the Great Clock Tower*, *The Herne's Egg*, *Purgatory* and *The Death of Cuchulain*. It follows Yeats' order of the plays, which is roughly the order of composition, the one major exception being the four Cuchulain plays *At the Hawk's Well*, *The Green Helmet*, *On Baile's Strand*, and *The Only Jealousy of Emer*, which are set out according to their narrative sequence and therefore suggest a natural grouping. Certain plays, such as *Where There is Nothing* or *Fighting the Waves*, are omitted and certain versions are preferred. Such choices can be enlightening and, with the help of *VPl*, critics range freely over the entire canon of Yeats' plays. A number of points should be noticed here. The text of *CK* in *CPl* is not the 1892 version but the fifth one, first published in 1919. Reading the two versions side by side in *VPl* enables us to see Yeats, in revising his favourite play, develop as a dramatist. The revisions to *SW*, which Yeats began in 1894, repay study; the 1900 version can be found in *VPl*, the 1906 version in *CP*, the 1907 Acting Version in *CPl* (the reference to 1911 is misleading), and the MS in Sidnell, Mayhew, Clark (1971). For critical discussion of these texts Parkinson (1951), Bushrui (1965) and Miller (1977) are worth referring to. The Cornell Yeats is devoted to manuscript materials and scheduled to run for 25-30 volumes. The series began with *The Death of Cuchulain* (see Yeats, 1982), and has continued with *P* (Yeats, 1984) and *The Early Poetry Volume 1: 'Mosada' and 'The Island of Statues'* (Yeats, 1987). Although outside Yeats' own preferred canon, *Where There is Nothing*, which has recently been published with *The Unicorn From the Stars* (see Yeats and Lady Gregory, 1987), gives valuable insights into the playwright's radical and Nietzschean vision that where there is nothing, there is God. Bradford (1965), who also edited the MS of *The Player Queen* (1971), provides information about the changes in composition to *At the Hawk's Well*, *The Words upon the Window Pane*, *The Resurrection*, *A Full Moon in March*, and *Purgatory*. He makes the point that Yeats' procedure in writing plays was similar to the poetry beginning with a 'prose' draft, a 'scenario', or a vision of dramatic action. Bradford also notices how Yeats' apprenticeship as a dramatist ended with *GH* (1910); after 1910 he rarely rewrote his plays.

Yeats' own essays on drama, together with his introductions and notes to his plays, should not be neglected, since his ideas – his theory – are central to any study. See, especially, the section entitled 'The Irish Dramatic Movement: 1901-1919' in *Ex*, 'The Cutting of an Agate' (1912) in *E & I*, the prefaces and introductions in *VPl* (pp. 1288-1312), *Samhain* (Yeats, 1970), the theatre magazine he edited from 1901 to 1908 (some of whose essays appear in *Ex*), *Beltaine* (Yeats, 1970a), the organ of the Irish Literary Theatre which Yeats edited in 1899-1900. Among the bench-mark essays are 'Certain Noble Plays of Japan' (*E & I*, pp. 221-37), 'The Tragic Theatre' (*E & I*, pp. 238-45), and 'A People's Theatre: A Letter to Lady Gregory' (*Ex*, pp. 244-62).

Yeats' Theatre

The poet in the theatre

If the Irish literary revival had its origins in a language revival, then the key date is 1893, the year that witnessed the founding of the Gaelic League and the publication of Hyde's *Love Songs of Connacht*. The Gaelic League, with branches throughout Ireland, was dedicated to promoting Irish and to what its President Hyde in 1894 called 'the necessity of de-anglicising Ireland' (Hyde, 1894). In translating the Gaelic songs, Hyde pioneered a more natural rendering of Hiberno-English, and laid the foundations for the work of Synge and Lady Gregory. While Yeats never learned Irish, he was constantly exposed to the cultural forces proclaiming Ireland's difference, especially in its use of language. There are many contexts to Yeats' work as a poet in the theatre, including the Irish Dramatic Movement, his antipathy to Ibsen and naturalism, his development as a poet, his involvement in the occult, the idea of poet as mage, and the English Aesthetic Movement. But we should not forget the language revival; Yeats' attention to language reveals not only his links with the Irish language revival of the 1890s but also his own commitment to the political and cultural necessity of de-anglicising Ireland.

Yeats' work as a poet in the theatre is normally discussed in terms of literary form and the place of poetry in modern drama as a whole. It was this aspect that Eliot focused on in his 1940 lecture on Yeats, commenting in turn on the development of Yeats' lyric and dramatic poetry, and judiciously concluding that Yeats is not only a lyric and dramatic poet but is also 'the type of lyrical dramatist' (Eliot, 1940). Peacock (1946) begins his inquiry into the relations between poetry and the theatre in modern European literature with Eliot, 'whose work illumines retrospectively most of the problems of the whole period'. As to Yeats, Peacock defends him against the charge that his plays are more lyrical than dramatic and cites *The Dreaming of the Bones*, a play whose 'emotion is the most fanatic Irish patriotism'. Peacock finds in Yeats' upholding of convention and formality, especially in speech, movement, stage-setting and music, a link with Goethe and the Greeks. In terms of subject-matter Yeats broke new ground in exploring 'complex and subtle mental worlds'. He extended the use of symbolism beyond what had been familiar in European drama since the 16th century and made it dominate his 'actions' so that his symbolism 'makes explicit the universality of the theme'. Thus Yeats' plays are concerned not so much with personal lyrical states of mind as great themes. Further discussion of this subject can be found in Nicoll (1949) and Donoghue (1959).

The Abbey Theatre

For a more complete understanding of Yeats' drama it is important to know something about the 'theatres' for which he wrote, in particular the Abbey Theatre and the traditional Japanese Noh drama. Yeats' interest in drama began in the 1880s when four of his dramatic poems were published – *The Island of Statues* in 1885, *Mosada* in 1886, *Time and the Witch Vivien* in 1889 and *WO* the same year. It was further kindled by Florence Farr's performance in Todhunter's *A Sicilian Idyl*, which he saw while living in Bedford Park in 1890. Then in 1892 came *CK*, to be followed by *The Land of Heart's Desire* in 1894. But he lacked an audience for his work. As he wrote in his note to *ATHW* in 1916, which can also be applied to this early period, 'I need a theatre; I believe myself to be a dramatist' (*VPl*, p. 415). In 1898 an opportunity arose when he and Lady Gregory met at Duras, the home of Edward Martyn in Kinvara, County Galway. In the letter they circulated to potential subscribers to the project – 'We propose to have performed in Dublin...' (see Lady Gregory, 1913) – they set out their high ideals and intentions. Their remarks reveal the ideological conjuncture that existed on the eve of the creation of a national theatre in Ireland. The originators were high-minded, intent on staging Irish plays in Dublin in the spring of each year – 'Celtic' acknowledges the 1890s note and suggests the wider British gallery to which they also played. The audience was to be an uncorrupted one with a passion for oratory, and against the stage Irishman and the view of the Celt propounded by Arnold (1867), 'sentimental – always ready to react against the despotism of fact', they invoked an ancient idealism (Yeats' 'bardic' tone is heard throughout the passage). Against the English commercial theatre they proposed an experimental theatre (Irish idealism versus English materialism). They hoped that culture would be a unifying force above politics (according to Yeats, the fall of Parnell in 1890 permitted a breathing-space for the rise of literature).

Such a 'manifesto', alert as it is to the signals in culture and society, is deliberately interventionist, but it uncannily betrays all the points of future tension. Firstly, while the authors stressed freedom to experiment and Irishness, they little imagined that their project would be funded by an Englishwoman, Annie Horniman, who was to take exception to many of their decisions (see Fay (1958) or Robinson (1942,1951)). Secondly, contention plagued the Abbey: a rumbling dispute, for example, between the high-minded (often seen as high-handed) 'Anglo-Irish' Directors and the rest of the Company led in 1906 to the formation of the Theatre of Ireland and in 1908 to the departure of the Fay brothers – for an inside view of the breakaway theatre company, see Nic Shiubhlaigh (1955). Thirdly, neither the audience nor the press were noted for tolerance, as the *Playboy* riots of 1907 remind us; fourthly, the exclusive insistence on Irish plays and on an idealism bordering on isolationism ran counter to the rising star of naturalism. Finally, the work of new playwrights such as 'the Cork realists' Murray, Robinson and Ray (Robinson, 1942), or others such as Boyle, Colum and O'Kelly, produced an Irish dramatic movement very different from that envisaged by Yeats.

Early surveys of the Abbey can be found in Lady Gregory (1913), Boyd (1922), Malone (1929) and Fay and Carswell (1935); later surveys include Ellis-Fermor (1939), Robinson (1951), Fay (1958), McCann (1967), O hAodha (1974), Flannery (1976), Miller (1977), and Maxwell (1984); a year-by-year account of the period from 1899 to 1910 is provided by Hogan and Kilroy (1975 and 1978) and Hogan, Burnham, and Poteet (1979). Though still useful, Ellis-Fermor's account of the Irish dramatic movement affords a cautionary tale, especially in her assumption that it *was* a movement, and in her elevation of Yeats. She writes in her preface, 'I sometimes think that I began to write a book about the Irish Dramatic movement and ended by writing a book on Yeats', but this can be misleading, because a movement requires many things: playwrights, companies, finance, buildings, an audience and a cultural context. It would be more accurate to say that Yeats is not the only key figure in the development of modern Irish drama, that he was only partly successful, that his own ideas for the theatre never fully materialised and that in a sense he never had his own theatre for his plays. Most of the plays staged by the Abbey Theatre in its first ten years (1904-14) did not comply with Yeats' theory of drama; most of the playwrights explored realistic, often Ibsenesque, themes such as the power of the clergy, the subdivision of the land, the issues of inheritance or emigration. These plays did exhibit a 'return to the people', which Yeats had advocated (*Samhain*, October 1902, p. 9), but they were not designed to 'uplift the man of the roads' and their language was not poetry.

With chapters on the *Playboy* riots in Dublin, the defiant staging of Shaw's *The Shewing Up of Blanco Posnet* (1910) after its ban in England, and the *Playboy* troubles in America in 1911, Lady Gregory (1913) reminds us of the courage it took to establish 'Our Irish Theatre' (note the proprietorial tone). Her remarks on her co-operation with Yeats in writing *Cathleen ni Houlihan* or her comment that 'it is the existence of the Theatre that has created play-writing among us' reveal her quiet assurance and suggest the part she played in the development of Yeats' drama, in particular his use of dialogue. But because it concentrates on public skirmishes with prejudice and the authorities, her study is less intimate than some critics assume.

Robinson's slightly whimsical but informative study (1951) is the official history of the Abbey, which had its beginnings in the Irish Literary Theatre of 1899-1901, W.G. Fay's National Dramatic Society and later the Irish National Theatre Society of 1902-3. Robinson traces the evolution of the Abbey Theatre from its formation in 1904 through to 1951. He makes good use of contemporary documents and recollections. For those with a more specialised interest, he includes dates and casts of all first productions and brief biographies of leading playwrights. It is, however, difficult to gauge from this account Yeats' particular contribution as a playwright and for that we must go elsewhere. In his autobiography (1942), Robinson tells us that Yeats had 'an unerring eye for a situation', knew exactly the point of attack, and worked hard at revising his plays. Never mean, though never effusive, he ends appropriately with Yeats: 'From the day I met him to the day of his death he was the dominant personality in my life'.

Frank and Willie Fay present us with a very different picture of Yeats and the Abbey. For them the Abbey was 'first and foremost a theatrical, not a literary movement'. While Ibsen made a theatre to suit his plays, in Ireland the Abbey was made first, and only afterwards were plays got to suit it. Included in this study is a record of the events leading up to Willie Fay's resignation from the Theatre in 1908. This is pursued in Fay (1958), a study which also emphasises the practical and financial aspects of the Theatre, the early contact in August 1901 between the Fays and Yeats and the various disputes, rows and resignations.

The Fays' contribution to the Abbey is assessed in Nic Shiubhlaigh (1955), in Fallon's essay in McCann (1967), which includes a discussion of Antoine, Stanislavsky and Coquelin, as well as some remarks on Yeats and the actor, and in Flannery (1976). Holloway in his enthralling, gossipy and often savage diary (1967) invariably supports the Fays in their disputes with the Directors, but even he has to admit that five months after their departure the performances were still excellent. 'Theatre business, management of men' (a line from 'The Fascination of What's Difficult' written 1909-10) conveys in its collocation of theatre with business, and of theatre business with management of men, Yeats' increasing frustration with administering the Abbey. 'The Abbey Theatre will fail to do its full work because there is no accepted authority to explain why the more difficult pleasure is the nobler pleasure', he writes in *Estrangement*, his 1909 diary (*A*, p. 491).

For briefer accounts of Yeats and the Abbey, it is worth referring to the authoritative O hAodha (1974), Tuohy (1976), and Saddlemyer's essay 'Worn Out With Dreams: Dublin's Abbey Theatre' in Skelton and Saddlemyer (1965). Flannery (1976) and Miller (1977) provide the fullest and most perceptive accounts of

Yeats in the context of the Abbey Theatre. In his introduction Flannery claims that Yeats' 'dramatic theories are more important than his actual practices' and that his basic struggle is to reconcile theory with practice. He sites that struggle in 'the dialectic of opposites that raged within his personality', the shy child who sought his opposite in athletes, passionate men, heroic dreams and the Mask. The younger Yeats sought an ideal beyond life, which made him emotionally vulnerable; this in turn led to immersion in practical theatre and the occlusion of the subjective self. Flannery explores this fundamental theme of his work – 'the war of the spiritual with the natural order' (SR, p. vii) – and shows how it surfaces through his interests in folklore, the occult and nationalism. He outlines the European, English and Irish contexts, comparing Yeats with Wagner, Maeterlinck and the Symbolists. He touches on the success and failure of the Irish literary theatre and on Yeats' realisation that after the Church's attack on *CK* in the 1890s he needed to propagandise for a new theatre. But Yeats was also interested in fostering a poetical culture, where there was a place, on the one hand, for passion, musical speech and everything embodied in the figure of the Dancer, and on the other hand for both occult ritual and aesthetic pattern. Flannery traces Yeats' relationship with Craig and suggests that it was Craig and not Pound who introduced Yeats to the Noh drama. Certainly the title of his journal (*The Mask*) cannot be overlooked in assessing Yeats' own formulation of his ideas about the Mask and the anti-self in these same years of his association with Craig. Further discussion of Yeats and Craig can be found in essays by Flannery and Dorn in O'Driscoll and Reynolds (1975) and in Dorn (1984). It is also worth tracking down a copy of Yeats' *Plays For An Irish Theatre* (1911); the designs by Craig are a visible link between Irish material and avant-garde experimentalism.

On Yeats as a dramatist, Flannery (1976) stresses the autobiographical imprint and the need for self-dramatisation, but also how this is qualified by an awareness of character in action. He comments on Lady Gregory's influence, on the revisions to *SW*, *On Baile's Strand* and *The Hour-Glass*, and on what the revisions reveal about Yeats' stature as a poetic dramatist. He reminds us that Yeats' development as a dramatist was not a continuous evolution. In concluding chapters on Yeats as a manager and on his legacy as a dramatist, Flannery observes that the Abbey's younger writers rejected the peasant quality ('pq' as it was sometimes known) and that in 1919 Yeats may have felt discouraged and defeated, although by that date the Abbey had produced 130 new Irish plays. The Abbey has been the inspiration of writers, painters and revolutionaries, and its influence can still be felt in independent theatres throughout Britain and North America. Yeats has yet to receive his 'due recognition', but, with the influence of Grotowski and Brook, a major re-evaluation is in sight.

Miller's study (1977) has carefully chosen illustrative material from the early productions, including Yeats' sketches for his plays, costumes by Ricketts and Dulac, musical settings by Elgar, Farr and Antheil, set designs by Craig, book designs by Moore, Beardsley's poster for *The Land of Heart's Desire*, woodcuts by Craig and Elinor Monsell, and masks by Krop for the 1922 Amsterdam production of *The Only Jealousy of Emer*. For Miller, Yeats is a man of the theatre whose plays are 'informed by an instinct for theatre practice which...has not been equalled by any other great dramatic poet for centuries past'. Indeed, the Irish National Theatre is 'largely Yeats' creation'. Unlike Flannery, Miller tracks his subject play by play. This is perhaps the most complete account of Yeats' theatre work, and there emerges a portrait of a remarkable person who was by turns co-founder and director of a theatre, fundraiser and propagandist (see *Beltaine* and *Samhain*), as well as a fully-committed playwright, the author of 26 plays, including poetic dramas, folk-plays, heroic dramas, plays for dancers and Noh-inspired plays. He experimented with collaboration with Moore over *Diarmuid and Grania* (1901), and was actively engaged with the form of drama, with acting and speech, music and dance, costumes and colours, stage setting and design. He was also alive to new ideas and experiments, often outside Ireland, a point that Miller makes by default. The Irish literary theatre began, according to Miller, when Yeats saw a performance of *Axel* in Paris in February 1894; his debt to Craig dates from a production of *Dido and Aeneas* in Notting Hill Gate in 1901. Only in London, as he writes in his introduction to *Certain Noble Plays of Japan* (1916), could he find the help he needed in constructing a framework for his dramatic ideas, and ironically, many of his middle plays were not performed in Dublin until some time after they were written: *ATHW* in 1933, *The Only Jealousy of*

Emer in 1926, *The Dreaming of the Bones* in 1931. On two occasions they were staged under the auspices of the Dublin Drama League. This contains a further irony, because the Dublin Drama League, an offshoot of the Abbey, was inspired by Martyn's internationalism, an outlook which had earlier brought him into conflict with Yeats' theories. Miller, however, tends to gloss over the awkward passages in Yeats' career as an Irish dramatist and to avoid altogether the issue of discontinuity.

'An unpopular theatre'

When the Noh-inspired *ATHW* was produced in Lady Cunard's London drawing-room on 2 April 1916, advanced nationalists in Dublin were finalising their plans for the Easter Rising on 24 April. This juxtaposition reminds us of Yeats' different theatres; one in his early career which was populist and oriented towards the public stage and the Irish people (he was in later life to wonder 'Did that play of mine send out/Certain men the English shot'); the other was elitist, small-scale and more properly private. By 1919, the 'People's Theatre' had become 'a discouragement and a defeat...I want to create for myself an unpopular theatre and an audience like a secret society where admission is by favour and never to many'. (*Ex*, pp. 250-4). One aspect of this change of heart concerns the influence of the Noh on his middle and later plays.

The part Pound played in Yeats' development has often been discussed. Longenbach (1988) sets this in the modernist context (see p. 129 below), while Litz stresses the personal nature of the friendship. Litz (1985) focuses on the period immediately preceding the winter of 1913-14, the first of three winters Yeats and Pound were together at Stone Cottage in Sussex. Their friendship began with Pound's ambition when he arrived in England in 1908 to meet the greatest living poet. Pound was encouraged by Yeats' ability to leave behind the shadows of the 1890s, but in 1911-12 he developed a more critical attitude, and by early 1913 he felt that Yeats was 'wavering between two poetic worlds'. Before going to Stone Cottage, Pound wrote that 'Yeats will amuse me part of the time and bore me to death with psychical research the rest', but, exposed to Yeats' generosity, he revised this opinion. Ellmann (1970) summarises the biographical and critical connections between them, touching on Pound's 'role in the modernization of Yeats'. Pound helped Yeats clarify *ATHW* and he was responsible for finding Michio Ito, a Japanese dancer who played the Guardian of the Well in *ATHW*. Ellmann also notices the way they 'face each other in an unended debate'. Diggory (1983) discusses their mutual influence; how they differed in their understanding of tradition; how Pound's dissociation from Yeats began in 1913; how, for Yeats, 'Mauberley' was a document of self-discovery whereas for Pound it was an anti-confessional poem, and how Pound rediscovered the subjective vision in *The Pisan Cantos*. After Stone Cottage, Yeats turned increasingly to the East, though we should not assume this was because of Pound. It is always difficult to disentangle debt from corroboration in Yeats, but he was probably confirmed in this direction by Pound. Interestingly, the first sign of this renewed awakening to the East surfaced not in his verse but in his drama, with *ATHW*, the first of *Four Plays for Dancers*.

In his introduction to Fenollosa's volume (1916) Yeats suggested that with the help of Japanese plays translated by Fenollosa and Pound he had invented 'a form of drama, distinguished, indirect, and symbolic, and having no need of mob or Press to pay its way – an aristocratic form' (*E & I*, p. 221). When writing *ATHW*, Yeats had available in translation fewer than 20 of the 250 or so extant Noh plays, a reminder that he did not feel inhibited by slender knowledge of a subject. At the same time, in distinguishing what he knew from what he made of the Noh theatre, we should not assume that his errors are 'portals of discovery' or that he sought accuracy in translation. Characteristically, Yeats always develops the form he is using. For those interested in the Noh *per se*, Fenollosa (1916) or Waley (1920) contain examples of different types of plays and remarks on the history and ideas of the Noh theatre. Some of Waley's observations strike immediate chords for the student of Yeats (compare, for example, p. 53 (1920) with the Yeatsian concept of Dreaming Back).

For discussion of Yeats and the Noh from a Japanese point of view, see Ishibashi (1968) and Komesu (1984). Ishibashi's overall aim is to describe the ideal of beauty pursued in Noh and how this compares with Yeats. In a wide-ranging, if slightly disjointed survey, he makes a number of distinct observations. The Noh, which flourished at the conjuncture of two cultures, the age of the nobles and that of the warriors, established itself in the aesthetic tradition of the first but its mode of representation belongs to the second. Various types of beauty are displayed in the Noh, one of which is Yugen or Ideal Beauty. Of the two types of expression one is mild and leaves something out of account, the other is the expression of a fleeting and intense emotion. There are no deformed persons in the Noh, who are accommodated in Kyogen, a form Yeats had in mind when he wrote *The Cat and the Moon*. Comparison between Yeats and the Noh can be briefly summarised. Yeats believed that the secret of the Noh lay in stylization, unity of images and concentration, but he lacked an overall idea of beauty and mixed types. In the Noh, elements in the play are subordinated to the Main Player, whereas in Yeats the drama turns on two characters in conflict. In the Noh, players do not evoke strangeness; instead, the audience is invited to participate in the events on stage. A character on stage can undergo marked changes, the Noh being freer here than Yeats. The setting for a Noh play is normally the present and the place part of the natural world. When a ghost appears this is because of its attachment to a person or a place. Ishibashi notes that between the chorus in a Yeats play and a Noh play there is no resemblance, and he generously concludes that Yeats 'created an entirely new form' of the Noh.

Taylor (1976) provides a full-length, though somewhat hesitant, study of the relationship between Irish myth and Japanese Noh, which does, however, illuminate certain aspects of Yeats' debt. Yeats' interest is contextualised by reference to *Japonisme* in the period 1865-95, to the work of Fenollosa and to the small auditorium – the one lesson Yeats learnt from the clubhouse theatre in his Bedford Park days. The outline of a Noh play is discussed in detail: the place of the *shite* (central figure) and the *waki* (interlocutor); the various groupings of Noh plays by subject-matter and emotional experience. He also discusses examples from the plays in the modern repertoire. In dealing with specific plays by Yeats, Taylor makes a number of points: the relevance of *Aoi no Ue* for an understanding of *The Only Jealousy of Emer*; the debt of *The Dreaming of the Bones* to *Nishikigi*; the differences between *Four Plays for Dancers* and the Noh; the way *The Death of Cuchulain* is Yeats' most Noh-like play. In an essay elsewhere Taylor comments on the Noh source for *ATHW* (O'Driscoll and Reynolds, 1975). But the issue of whether the Noh was crucial to Yeats' development as a dramatist – or simply a catalyst and confirmation – remains unresolved.

Yeats' Plays

The Cuchulain cycle

Yeats wrote five plays in what is sometimes called the Cuchulain cycle of plays. In order of composition they are: *On Baile's Strand* (1904), *GH* (1908), *ATHW* (1916), *The Only Jealousy of Emer* (1919), and *The Death of Cuchulain* (1938); but if set out according to the story of Cuchulain's life, the order would need to be adjusted. Because it presents itself as a natural grouping or genre, a view supported by the plays' arrangement in *CPl* (1934), such a cycle cuts across chronological surveys of Yeats' plays, and can throw a different light on how we read or group them. The importance of Cuchulain for the Irish literary revival stems from the work of O'Grady (1878, 1881 and 1894). His historical accounts and imaginative recreation ensured that the ancient Irish hero from the Red Branch cycle of stories became the key mythological figure. So much so that in 'The Statues' Yeats imagined Cuchulain during the Easter Rising stalking with Pearse through the Post Office. But the more immediate source for Yeats' cycle can be found in Lady Gregory's *Cuchulain of Muirthemne* (1902). This book's charm resides principally in its 'Kiltartanese' dialect, for Lady Gregory with Hyde (1893) and Synge transformed in their different ways the literary possibilities for Hiberno-English. Yeats described it, in a phrase that Stephen Dedalus mocks in *Ulysses*, as 'the best [book] that has come out of Ireland in my time' (Lady Gregory, 1902, p. 11).

Yeats' Cuchulain cycle has been approached from several different angles: through changes to source material, the question of unity and other factors including the autobiographical imprint and the significance of Cuchulain for Yeats himself. Friedman (1977), 'traces the playwright's progress towards psychodrama', from the imitator of Shakespeare in *On Baile's Strand* to the 'finisher of the myth of the innermost self' in *The Death of Cuchulain*. Short accounts can be found in Ure (1963a), Hoffman (1967) and Moore (1971), but here I concentrate on full-length studies by Bjersby (1950) and Skene (1974). Bjersby (1950), who appends a useful summary of the Red Branch cycle of stories, examines the sources for both the poems and plays that deal with Cuchulain. 'Death of Cuchulain' echoes Ferguson's poem 'Fergus Wry-Mouth'; *On Baile's Strand* owes most to Lady Gregory in her chapter 'The Only Son of Aoife' (1902); the source for *GH* is Lady Gregory again, only now Yeats treats the material more as comedy than tragedy; *ATHW* and *The Only Jealousy of Emer*, which also belong to another series of plays, namely *Four Plays for Dancers*, present striking similarities with the Noh; 'Cuchulain Comforted' arose from a dream he had on 7 January 1939, while *The Death of Cuchulain* shows Yeats transforming the source in Lady Gregory. In the second chapter, on 'Drama-Life', Bjersby stresses the autobiographical nature of the plays and traces, for example, the events surrounding the composition of *The Only Jealousy of Emer*. A final chapter on Yeats' life-view includes reference to the insight Yeats' prose gives to his drama, to the magical elements in the plays (superstition in *On Baile's Strand*, landscape in *GH*, the well in *ATHW*, and the world of the spirits in *The Only Jealousy of Emer*) and to the influence of the System on the later plays; how the idea of Phases is already apparent in *The Only Jealousy of Emer*, and how *The Death of Cuchulain* incorporates the Great Wheel. In her conclusion Bjersby suggests that the Cuchulain cycle presents Yeats in three aspects, as Poet, Man and Interpreter of Life, and that his style and ideas show a gradual evolution.

Skene (1974) could have made more of his practical knowledge gained from producing the five plays in a single evening, especially as he stresses that they form 'a coherent and unified play cycle'. The first half of his book – on the contexts for the plays – is invaluable, though the second half – on the plays themselves – is less interesting. Skene posits that the Cuchulain plays are part of Yeats' desire to regenerate Ireland by means of an Irish mystical order, and he cites Yeats' remark in a letter to Sturge Moore: 'I always feel that my work is not drama but ritual of a lost faith' (Yeats, 1953, p. 156). Included in this ritual are landscape, legend and the occult. The cycle from *ATHW* to *The Death of Cuchulain* is 'intensely personal, yet [it] somehow embraces the story of Ireland'. Skene next discusses the differences between Lady Gregory (1902) and the plays themselves, and shows how the Cuchulain plays belong to the Celtic Revival. He also relates the plays to *AV* and imagines the Cuchulain cycle in the shape of a wheel with individual plays corresponding to different phases. The Cuchulain cycle is then interpreted as 'the story of the romance between the Sun and the Moon', 'keyed to their function as seasonal ritual' with plays associated with different points of the seasonal cycle. The fourth chapter brings together the plays and Yeats' own life, and shows Yeats identifying with Cuchulain for his 'creative joy separated from fear' (L, 913). For example, the emotional power of *ATHW* derives from Yeats' devotion to Maud Gonne, the twin forces in his life at this time being sexual desire and commitment to an heroic life, while *The Only Jealousy of Emer* belongs to the period when Yeats proposed marriage to three different women, Maud Gonne, Iseult Gonne and Georgina Hyde-Lees, and the power of *The Death of Cuchulain* arises from its being completed a few weeks before his death. In his fifth chapter Skene explores Yeats' ideas on production. In his discussion of specific plays, useful insights are made. He likens *ATHW* to an initiation ceremony in which Cuchulain accepts his hawk nature, his tragic destiny and the heroic commitment on which that destiny is based; the Fool and the Blind Man in *On Baile's Strand* adumbrate the other plays in the cycle. Equally, when the plays are read or seen as a group, the dominant images – the hawk, the cat-heads, the flames, the waves – become more apparent.

Last plays

Wilson (1958) offers a difficult starting-point for an examination of the last five plays. He sets out his particular stall in the introduction: with the New Critics in his sights, he claims that Yeats' poetry requires an ulterior body of knowledge – heterodox mysticism – and the reader's sympathy for such ideas. He outlines Yeats' subjective philosophy and his attraction to inherited symbolism and the doctrine of correspondence. He notices that Yeats' early symbolism has medieval roots, and that the work of Porphyry, whom he began reading in 1895, becomes increasingly important. He also comments on how the Noh, with its assertion of traditional symbolism and the return to religion it afforded, became the model for his mature drama. According to Wilson, the negative criticism often levelled against the last plays can be offset if people are conversant with the neo-Platonic tradition of Western thought. Wilson then examines each play in turn. *The King of the Great Clock Tower* is a reconstruction of the Platonic myth of the relation between matter and spirit, while *A Full Moon in March* illustrates the Platonic theory of opposites; in this case heaven is incomplete in its separation from humanity. In *The Herne's Egg* he detects a movement from Platonism to Pythagoras and the *Upanishads*; from Indian religion Yeats derived the belief that the pure self is identical with God and also that India and ancient Ireland are complementary. This play is difficult for three reasons; its philosophy, its symbolism and the oblique literary allusions. *P*, which Yeats considered a ghost play, is an essay in the psychology of the supernatural, combining a treatise on the Platonic theory of the 'body of air' with a bitter commentary on the collapse of aristocratic Ireland. Wilson observes that Yeats' concepts of Return and Dreaming Back preceded both his study of oriental philosophy and his wife's automatic writing and belong to 1914-15 when he was reading the Cambridge Platonists and Swedenborg. Finally, *The Death of Cuchulain*, a play about the death-wish, where, in Yeats' own words we 'die each other's life' (*L*, p. 917), is an 'odd fusion of the Platonic and the Gaelic', being an interpretation of an Irish myth via Platonic philosophy.

In a subsequent study, Wilson (1960) examines the symbolism in *Four Plays for Dancers* and *The Cat and the Moon* and suggests that each of the five plays embodies an aspect of Yeats' metaphysics. *ATHW* is concerned with the religion of the Self, *The Only Jealousy of Emer* with reincarnation, *Calvary* with objectivity, *The Dreaming of the Bones* with life after death, and *The Cat and the Moon* with history. For Wilson what is valuable about Yeats is his theory of the Self and how it counters the historical development of Christianity towards objectivity. Both these studies by Wilson, and especially the first, have pioneered an approach towards Yeats that takes his occult interests seriously. Both emphasise the value of sources to an understanding of the plays and poems, the different ways Irish and other myths combine with such sources, the significance of the Noh theatre and the centrality of the supernatural, which cannot be relegated to a side issue with Yeats. In clarifying these sources Wilson makes a useful contribution to our reading of Yeats, but by stressing the ideas of his chosen tradition he risks losing sight of the practical Yeats who involved himself in automatic writing and gravitated towards ceremonial magic rather than mysticism: in his discussion of *The Only Jealousy of Emer*, for example, there is no mention of Iseult

Gonne. This display of erudition also provokes the thought either that the plays are too difficult to be understood or that the erudition is excessive and the plays can be better appreciated for what they are, namely drama!

Vendler (1963) takes a different tack: to understand the later plays it is necessary to understand *AV*, but *AV* as conceived in aesthetic and not esoteric terms. For Vendler, *AV* has its origins in the symbolic Rose of the 1890s and is concerned with poetry rather than philosophy. It centres on symbolism in poetry, the relationship between poet and Muse, how the Muse operates, the movement of literary history, and what constitutes the subject-matter of poetry. Thus Book I of *AV* deals with literary history, Book II poetic creation, Book III poetic activity, Book IV the imagination shaping history and Book V the Muse. Vendler explores each of these in turn, noticing *inter alia* that Book V is a commentary on 'Leda and the Swan' and that Yeats' historical formulations are 'nonsense at worst and wildly intuitive guesses at best' – a view that supports her own aesthetic interpretation. On specific plays, Vendler comments on the difficulty of writing about *The Player Queen* because the characters melt into each other and because, even though the germinal idea is tragic, the vision of cataclysm is ironic. With regard to *The King of the Great Clock Tower, A Full Moon in March* and *The Herne's Egg* and the singing and dancing consequent upon death, Vendler declares that she is 'uncomfortable with any view imputing mystical references to Yeats' plays, and consequently prefer[s] to think that the theological symbols...have primarily aesthetic and human reference'. In her chapter 'Plays of Death, Purgation, and Resurrection' she distinguishes this view more explicitly from Wilson. For Wilson, Yeats found the themes for such plays in esoterica, but for Vendler 'Yeats sought out esoteric doctrines about the afterlife because his imagination was already obsessed with the afterlife as symbol'. Death and purgation are allied therefore with the creative function, but Vendler concedes that discussing *P* as a parable of the imagination is 'thin and unsatisfying'. She also interprets the Cuchulain cycle in terms of the imagination, but again finds nothing is gained by translating *ATHW* into aesthetic terms, although *The Death of Cuchulain*, a play she calls a 'rough draft', does support her thesis. In conclusion Vendler returns to the way primary questions of *AV* are taken up by the plays: 'how do we account for the perpetual vigour of the imagination, and how should we react in the presence of an obsolete poetic tradition?'.

Vendler and Wilson provide sharply contrasting and challenging, if one-sided, interpretations of Yeats' last plays. Other critics pursue different courses. Good (1987) takes issue with Vendler, whom she claims ignores the tragic dimension to Yeats' plays. In his early Cuchulain plays Yeats was searching for a new mode of presentation, a mode of dramatising mythic truth where the hero finds revelation in the tragic moment. *Four Plays for Dancers* concentrate on the instant of tragic recognition, illustrate the doctrine of ideal beauty and reveal a bleak psychological landscape; the three aspects of Yeats' experience of tragedy. But in these plays, Good perceptively adds, Yeats is not writing tragedy so much as writing *about* it. Good then discusses *AV* and stresses four ideas central to the tragic vision: apocalypse, opposition of two states of being (Vision of Evil and Unity of Being), tragic encounter between the individual and his/her opposite and the cyclical nature of history. The drift of her argument here and elsewhere underlines Yeats' contrary vision of ultimate reality, how 'man is always confronted by his opposite; is doomed to lose what he loves; is thwarted and must finally encounter death'. *Calvary* and *Resurrection* centre on the panoramic vision of cyclical movement of time, while *The Words Upon the Window-Pane* and *P* deal with vision as 'dramatic experience' and ultimately with the Vision of Evil (Good's debt to Whittaker (1964) is acknowledged throughout). All this leads into a concluding discussion of the tragic joy as found in *The Death of Cuchulain*, the 'lonely figure of Cuchulain facing death'.

Clark's study (1965) is also helpful. Making use of the passion-purpose-perception triplet described by Kenneth Burke in *A Grammar of Motives*, Clark argues that Yeats' drama gravitates towards the moment of perception as the one moment of the tragic rhythm which provides a clue to life and action. The action of a typical Yeats play 'is not to demonstrate purpose or to express passion but to reveal perception'. Yeats' development as a dramatist was 'guided by his attempt to achieve a dramatic form and a dramatic-poetic speech suitable to this action of perception'. *Deirdre* presents not genuine tragic rhythm encoded in the triplet but 'the discovery that the first two are complementary parts of the third'. In *The Dreaming of the Bones* Yeats moves away from circumstantial realism and from depicting the struggle of purpose or the suffering of passion towards imitating 'the moment when passion becomes perception'. In *The Words Upon the Window-Pane*, where the too-solid world of actuality is rent by the spirit of Swift and the words upon the window pane 'carry us to the moment of perception', it is Ibsen, the great realist, who is excoriated by Yeats. *P*, with its 'achieved language of passionate perception', ends when nothing is left but the tragedy of vision. Clark's study devotes less time to the theme of 'desolate reality' than the title might suggest. As is often the case elsewhere in Yeats, there is an ambivalence about the phrase 'the desolation of reality' that appears in 'Meru', the source, presumably, for Clark's title. It is true that man's thought uproots only to find the desolation of reality, but the casual dismissal of the great civilisations of the past – 'Egypt and Greece good-bye, and good-bye, Rome!' – has the air of a rhetorical flourish in keeping with the poet who had written in 'The Tower' about 'Death and life were not/Till man made up the whole' and who was to write within five years of 'Meru' in 'The Statues' of those who 'put down/All Asiatic vague immensities'. It is not entirely clear in Clark what constitutes the desolate reality, for at least at one level it could be Ibsen's realistic world that is the focus of attack. Moreover, Clark's use of the Burke triplet also makes for problems in interpretation. As Ellison's *Invisible Man* (1952) reminds us, some of the best moments when the tragic rhythm in that novel can be felt occur during the period of passion and purpose, while the epilogue seems more like a pause than the anagnorisis or moment of genuine perception.

With special reference to the 'war of spiritual with natural order' (*SR,* p. vii) and how this is reflected in Yeats' actual plays, Nathan (1965) traces the evolution of Yeats' ideas about tragedy from the closet drama of *A Sicilian Idyl*, through the poetic theatre of *CK*, the aestheticism of *SW*, the tragicomedies of 1900-08, to the development of the anti-self in the period 1908-38. This is an original if slightly restricted study, carried through with commitment and intelligence. Nathan's chapter on the anti-self links the plays – perhaps too neatly – to the 28 Phases of the Moon, where Phases 8-22 constitute the subjective period, 23-7 the objective. The middle and last plays contain a spiritual conflict of opposites, but if the conflict occurs in the objective period, as is the case in *Calvary*, *Resurrection*, *The Dreaming of the Bones* and others, then no resolution is possible. This serves to contrast with the subjective group of plays, for example *ATHW*. *The Death of Cuchulain*, with its theme of 'the spiritual apotheosis of heroism at the very moment of the triumph of historical objectivity', falls into both groups. In another chapter where Nathan examines the influence of the Noh tradition, he slots the plays respectively into categories of subjective and objective tragedies. In a closing statement, Nathan suggests that 'Yeats' last plays restate, in a new way, the traditional position of tragedy: man, divided and complex, vulnerable both to the world and to himself, is forced to make choices that give him his destiny'. But, to my mind, the problem remains: can someone who believes in 'tragic joy' write tragedies?

Chapter 4

Yeats' Prose

Yeats as Story-teller

It can still surprise those who assume that 'Yeats' means the poet or the dramatist to learn that between 1887 and 1905 he edited four collections of fiction, wrote some twenty-three short stories and two novels, published six volumes of prose fiction – all this before he was 30. And yet, until quite recently, the situation in Yeats studies remained little different from that described in the 1930s when one commentator remarked that 'Yeats as a prose writer has...never been adequately treated, or, at any length' (Pollock, 1935). Fortunately, with the publication of Finneran (1973), Thuente (1980), O'Donnell (1983) and Putzel (1986), that situation is now being reversed, so that even studies not directly concerned with his fiction, such as Marcus (1970), Schricker (1982) or Kinahan (1988), are now attending to it as a matter of course. The contributions of Marcus (1970), Thuente (1980) and Kinahan (1988) are assessed in ch. 5 below, in Yeats and the Irish Context, which leaves room here to concentrate on O'Donnell, Finneran and Putzel.

O'Donnell (1983) provides the best short guide to Yeats' fiction. In introductory chapters he notices how Yeats was influenced in his decision to take up writing fiction by his father, his sister Elizabeth and the Rhymers; how his prose fiction contains two major elements – the use of folklore and the magical quest; how *SR* is a 'miscellany which does not even provide coherent chronological patterns'; and how Yeats is essentially a 'lyric artist' who could not handle extended narratives. Although he shunned technical innovation, Yeats placed considerable emphasis on craftsmanship. O'Donnell comments on the consciously poetic style of *John Sherman*, the uncertain handling of editorial commentary and on the clumsy narration of the final chapter, which confuses the novel's major theme. As to its autobiographical elements, O'Donnell takes issue with those critics like Ellmann (1948) who equate Sherman with Yeats or alternatively who see Sherman as the man and Howard the mask: Howard's character is humorous but he is neither a man of action nor a poet, nor is he someone Sherman can aspire to become. O'Donnell devotes two separate chapters to the stories of 1891-4 and 1895-6, commenting in turn on the sources, revisions and their relative strengths and weaknesses. 'Rosa Alchemica', 'The Tables of the Law' and 'The Adoration of the Magi' he sees as integral to *SR* in that they examine the attractions and liabilities of the 'supernal quest'. The first story combines the spiritual and the physical, ritual and passion, and its interpretation turns on the narrator's flight and whether or not this is praiseworthy. According to O'Donnell, it is the narrator and not the mystical Order which is indicted, for at stake is Yeats' pose of mirror-like indifference, his reluctance to surrender self-hood. The other two stories are less good, betraying structural weaknesses and an uninvolved narrator.

SB, whose four versions were written between 1896 and 1902, reflects the tension in Yeats between the demands for direct realism in the novel and the magus-like incantatory style of *WR* and *SW*. O'Donnell distinguishes between magus and artist and shows how Yeats began to accept a mid-position in the Cabalistic Tree of Life. *SB* is an extraordinary self-portrait and displays an unusual ability to accommodate contemporary personal action into fictional art. O'Donnell's discussion is brief, however, especially given the modern critical interest in unfinished texts, and for further analysis his edition of *SB* (1976) rewards attention. There O'Donnell outlines the differences between the four versions and reminds us of the autobiographical imprint in the text. *SB* is 'a spiritual autobiography...in the guise of a naturalistic novel'. The major characters in the 'final' version – Michael Herne, John Herne his father, Margaret Henderson, Samuel Maclagan, and Harriet St George – closely resemble Yeats himself, J.B. Yeats, Maud Gonne, MacGregor Mathers, and Olivia Shakespear, and the novel concerns Yeats' attempt to establish in Lough Key in County Roscommon the Castle of Heroes, an order of Celtic Mysteries, devoted to a religion of beauty, with Mathers supplying the ritual and Maud Gonne the beauty. Among the subjects dealt with are the father-son conflict, the nature of visionary experience, the isolation of the visionary from the ordinary world, the relationship between institutional Christianity, mysticism and the East, the disputes within the Order of the Golden Dawn and disappointment in love. *SB*'s location is the familiar geographical-psychological triangle that holds most of Yeats' early work; namely the west of Ireland, Paris and London.

Finneran (1973) provides a serviceable introduction to Yeats' prose fiction as a whole. *John Sherman* is particularly interesting for its autobiographical content. In *CT* Yeats 'wanted to both explain and justify his belief in the spiritual values inherent in the Irish landscape and the Irish peasantry' as well as to 'provide a storehouse of Irish folk and fairy material' for use both by himself and by later Irish writers. As to *SB*, Finneran discerns a combination of three kinds of prose fiction – legendary, realistic and esoteric – each of which Yeats had experimented with in the 1890s: in Book I there is the legendary, in Books II and IV the esoteric and occult, and in Book III the realistic. According to Finneran, Yeats' failure to complete the novel 'helped to bring about [his] abandonment of prose fiction'.

Putzel (1986) considers the unity of the first edition of *SR* (1897) and finds it contains the symbolic history of Ireland from the mythological era of the opening stories ('The Binding of the Hair' and 'The Wisdom of the King'), the Age of Saints and the Middle Ages ('Where There Is Nothing, There Is God' to 'Out of the Rose') and the 17th century ('The Curse of the Fires and of the Shadows' to 'Of Costello the Proud'), through the 18th century and the stories of Hanrahan, and finally to the last three stories which mark the end of two millennia. Putzel underlines the 'war of spiritual with natural order' (*SR*, p. vii) as well as the shifting perspectives on history – in *SR* history is seen as either sequence or apocalypse, and there exists a tension therefore between the diachronic and synchronic planes. He supports the unity of the volume. The final three stories, for example, are linked with the other stories via moods, motifs and images (e.g. spiritual fire, the serpent, the Rose), their view of history, the idea of personal quest and their fear of vision; they are connected with each other by the presence of a shared narrator, the common figure of Robartes and by their style. In the second half of his study Putzel explores the way *WR* presents the 'liturgy' of the symbolic system as outlined in *SR*, and in his conclusion suggests that *SR* provides the theoretical basis and the philosophical and historical context for

WR. This is a rewarding study which, building on the work of Kenner (1955), Grossman (1969) and others into the unity of individual volumes, widens the concept of unity by juxtaposing two cognate volumes published within two years of each other.

Yeats and Autobiography

A glance at recent titles will confirm that there has been considerable interest in Yeats and autobiography – see, for example, Ronsley (1968), Webster (1974), Perloff (1975), Ronsley (1977), Lynch (1979), Olney (1980a), O'Hara (1981), Lipking (1981), Allen (1982), Schricker (1982), Neuman (1982), Fletcher (1987) and Wright (1987). Taking their cue in part from the contemporary critical interest in the concept of the self, in part from the publication of *Memoirs* and other manuscript material, critics have felt free to wander over the whole corpus of Yeats' work in search of clues to his psyche. While no single study can represent every approach, many critics, in tracing Yeats' career as a writer, stress the final unity and the continuity of his achievement. But, with his distinction between character and personality, between the Primary and the Antithetical self, or with his Doctrine of the Mask and his characteristic dialectical mode, Yeats tantalises the modern critic in such a way that any study, even while it advances some kind of finality, is only as final, as 'temporary' that is, as its date of publication.

We can begin with Ronsley's brief and readable introduction to *A* (1968). His aim is to discover 'the design underlying Yeats' presentation of events, people, and ideas'. He comments on the fragmentariness of *R*, the possible influence of Joyce's *Portrait* with its disconnected narrative, on the significance of J.B. Yeats, and on the way the first volume of autobiography chronicles the development of three of Yeats' lifelong interests; namely mysticism, nationalism and art. In his discussion of *The Trembling of the Veil*, Ronsley foregrounds the concept of Unity of Being, shows how O'Leary and Taylor act as antithetical poles, how the artist's greatness is dependent on the conjunction of primary and antithetical, and how Yeats struggled to achieve unity via Ireland and the Great Memory. In *Dramatis Personae*, Yeats develops the idea of culture as reconciliation, how life and art, in Ronsley's words, 'had to be inseparable'. A similar approach can be found in Fletcher (1987), an essay originally published in Donoghue and Mulryne (1965). Fletcher, too, is concerned to detect the rhythm and pattern in *A*; the title of *R* signifies not an escape into the past but 'an attempt to distinguish pattern'. Fletcher comments on Yeats' process of mythologising both himself and the living, on Duffy as the anti-type of O'Leary, on the intellectual presentation of the father's crisis, and on Yeats' debt to Pater; this debt, especially evident in the recognition of the 'moment' as the unit of experience, Fletcher identifies in terms of attitude, not style. *The Trembling of the Veil* continues the process of mythologising, this time in the context of the 1890s generation of Dowson, Johnson and fellow Rhymers at the Cheshire Cheese. If *R* is a record of self-discovery via others, this volume adumbrates a new teleology, one which contains a sense of apocalypse counterposed by the symbol of Ireland.

Wright's study (1987), which includes a chart of the textual evolution of *A*, is a straightforward and unadventurous account of Yeats and autobiography. It contains, even so, some useful insights: firstly, the way Yeats challenges the formal definitions of genre and the assumptions often made about the relationship between author, text and reader; secondly, the relevance of *Portrait* to both *R* and *The Trembling of the Veil* (in *R* the terminal point comes when the protagonist acquires the ability to write books, while *Trembling* makes structural use of Parnell, and alternates between private and public in a movement outwards from the individual to the social); thirdly, the reasons for Yeats' retreat from commitment to self-revelation, which Wright ascribes to his reticence, his uncertainty in placing himself, his uneasiness about portraying characters at length and his mastery of self-portraiture in lyric form. Wright concentrates on the rhetorical strategies that 'draw us towards particular impressions of his life' and on how Yeats 'retains to the last a lively awareness of the complex interplay of his actual life, his imaginative accounts of his life, and his readers' responses to these accounts'. But Wright could have made more of the material at his disposal. The contrasts, for example, between Yeats and Joyce on autobiography are at least as promising as the similarities. Thus, making use of O'Hara's distinction (1981), we might notice how *R*, though initially seeming to conform to the pattern of Abrams' concept of the Romantic Spiral (the poet's internalised quest for creative significance), turns out to be better described by de Man's Deconstructive Labyrinth (the subversion of a genetic pattern of narrative development). *Portrait*, on the other hand, could be interpreted as working in the opposite direction, or from labyrinth to spiral.

Two books published in 1982 by Neuman and Allen offer differing views of the topic. Neuman (1982), which includes a valuable summary of the publishing history of *A*, counters the claim that Yeats achieved unity in his life. For some critics the change of title in 1938 from *Autobiographies* to *The Autobiography* indicates the final achievement of unity on Yeats' part (in passing, it is worth remembering that the former is used in the UK, the latter in the USA, and that different titles may contribute to different perceptions). For Neuman, however, such a change 'may have been motivated more by a desire to emphasise his intentions than by a personal conviction that he had realised himself apocalyptically for Yeats seems finally to have found life recalcitrant to his ideal of Unity of Being'. In discussing *The Bounty of Sweden*, Neuman comments on the way *A* 'charts the patterning of the self between two tensions; except for rare moments, they have not engendered and become one'. This is an insightful, occasionally cryptic book, which thrives on its unconventional readings. The central antithesis in *R*, Neuman maintains, is not between father and son but between the conflicting expressions of nationalism, especially in the figure of John F. Taylor; *A* is situated and reverberates between his poetry and his prose; Yeats' poetry does not so much illustrate his prose as resonate against it; *Estrangement*, with its denunciation of Irish politics and culture, seems not to belong in an autobiography; in *On the Boiler*, a text not normally associated with *A*, Yeats, in his acceptance of heroic defeat, takes to himself with unmediated directness and bitterness 'the heroic mind implied by the mythic structure of *Autobiographies*'.

This is also an appropriate point to comment on Allen (1982), which examines Yeats' epitaph in 'Under Ben Bulben' with a view to finding a 'key to symbolic unity in his life and work'. His first chapter on Yeats and Rilke, where he posits that the quatrain, 'Draw rein; draw breath./Cast a cold eye/On Life, on death./ Horseman pass by', was probably written before Yeats had read Rose's edition of Rilke's work, affords Allen a Pyrrhic victory only, for few readers are likely to think these lines restricted to Yeats' response to Rilke. Allen's chapter on Swift's epitaph, where he notices similarities between Yeats and Swift in their disdain for the middle class and their view of the cyclical or epochal nature of history, is more rewarding, especially in its focus on the question of who is addressed in the epitaph. Throughout this discussion a more general problem in Yeats can be felt; namely, the position of the reader in Yeats' texts, a problem rarely addressed by critics. In a chapter on the figure of the horseman, Allen favours an interpretation based on myth and traditional symbolism. Final chapters on Yeats' choice of Drumcliff Churchyard and on 'the two eternities' of race and soul complete Allen's study, though I am not fully persuaded that Yeats in his epitaph did hammer his thoughts into unity. That we can detect larger patterns at play in the epitaph, such as the presence of Yeats' paternal grandfather (as opposed to his maternal grandfather in *R*) should not blind us to the possibility that the epitaph marks not a conclusion, but only another milestone passed, whereby the finality of death is resisted.

Webster (1974) offers a somewhat raw, Freudian reading of Yeats. She traces the course of his life and work from its dreamy beginnings to the 'hard, concise richness and complexity of his late poems', and shows how the central thread of his life is his determination to remake himself, 'to bring himself as man and artist into a satisfactory relationship both with his impulses and with a threatening reality'. She assesses the questions of his mother's poor health and melancholia, and Yeats' identification with her 'female weakness'; the role of Laura Armstrong as an early stimulus for art and of Olivia Shakespear in the development of *SW*; the need for a woman to act as a source of emotional sustenance (fulfilled in part in his early career by Katharine Tynan); Lady Gregory's role as mother-provider; the association, at the time of *Where There is Nothing,* of the masculine ideal with destructiveness; the need to accept the body in 'Rosa Alchemica'; the significance of blood symbolism in Yeats' work; his obsession with death and how he coped with it by 'denial and gaiety'. The assumption throughout is that there is a 'real' Yeats behind the mask, that the 'real' autobiography, as it were, is contained not in *A* but in *Memoirs*. Such theoretical unsophistication – especially in the light of more recent deconstructionist and post-structuralist ideas – is exposed when Webster claims at one point that the process of symbol formation is the 'displacement of essential qualities from below the waist upward onto the head'. But Webster does raise important issues, and the topic of Yeats' relationship with women and his attitude towards femininity is returned to in the final chapter.

Arguing for the lyric as opposed to the dramatic Yeats, Schricker (1982) insists on his single identity and takes issue with those critics who assume the separation of character and personality, man and mask: 'Yeats' poetic "I" is securely grounded in autobiographical experience'. Thus *M* 'demonstrates a progressive development in Yeats' conception of the persona' from the barely augmented autobiographical presentation of *CT* to the part-fictional, part-autobiographical persona of 'Rosa Alchemica' to 'the artistically fully autonomous but empirically rounded thinking "I" ' of *PASL*. In her conclusion Schricker asserts that 'Yeats' poetic persona achieves that unity of being which the "great-rooted blossomer" of 'Among School Children' embodies'. If Webster errs on the side of reductionism, Schricker does so on the side of idealism, for if 'Among School Children' indicates anything, especially from what we know of the drafts, it is that rhapsody is the product of considerable intellectual effort and is rooted not in Unity of Being but in perception. If Yeats had achieved the state Schricker imagines, then the poem should by rights have concluded *T*; instead, it comes mid-way through the volume, and thus belongs to an argument about the 'artifice of eternity' of the opening poem, about the way that 'Death and life were not/Till man made up the whole', and about 'where the blessed dance' of 'All Souls' Night', the poem that concludes the volume. What is fascinating about 'Among School Children', apart from the way it changes course, is the dance of intellect and the fleeting vision of the unity of life. Neither of these aspects, however, should be confused with Unity of Being, a concept that is difficult to grasp without reference to a unity of culture – not a phrase that springs readily to mind in the context of Ireland in the 1920s.

Lynch (1979) rightly questions whether *R* is a faithful reflection of what took place in Yeats' childhood and suggests that Yeats' autobiography is told for the most part elsewhere than in his autobiographical volumes. Taking issue with the Oedipal reading of Yeats and autobiography, he proposes instead the narcissistic

Yeats, and reads a poem such as 'Among School Children' in terms of the indifference of Susan Pollexfen towards her son. Lynch finds support for this view in stanzas V and VII, especially in the contrast between the image the mother has of her son before he is born and 'her profound indifference to the son she bore'. The final stanza is interpreted as 'a rhetorical intimation of an idealised and ecstatic reunion of self and other that relieves the poet of the shameful burden of self-consciousness imposed by the maternal "image" '. There is a certain ingenuity, if not perversity, in such an argument. How do we know what Susan Pollexfen felt about her son either before or after he was born? Isn't stanza V sympathetic towards the mother and the question deliberately rhetorical? Doesn't the introduction of the mother highlight the ground the poet shares with that creator and observer of human life, who is not so much *his* mother as the representative of all mothers? It is difficult, in other words, to read this poem as a disguised account of the relationship between Yeats and his mother. This is not to say that Lynch is wrong in trying to illuminate this absence in the poet's life and work – only that the subject requires a more delicate touch, one that is alert to textual and intertextual surface features, especially those that resist being interpreted in biographical terms.

Taking his cue from the work of Ricoeur, O'Hara (1981) tries to steer a path between, on the one hand, the demystifying critical analysis in the genealogical style of Nietzsche, Freud and Heidegger and, on the other hand, the stress on creative recuperation evident in Hegel, Jung and Eliade. He stresses the place of irony in *A* and Yeats' progressive 'self-overcoming', particularly in the area of tragic knowledge. Tragic knowledge is the daimonic form of irony, a joyful acceptance on Yeats' part of his tragic fate as 'a member of a dying culture...playing with all the masks'. It is the ability to 'keep all moments in the total life process within the sphere of the imagination, for figurative enactment in one's work, and not for literal enactment...in the world'. From *R* through *The Trembling of the Veil* to *Dramatis Personae* and *Estrangement*, Yeats learns in turn how to confront the burden of the past, how to reconstruct its pattern, and how to deconstruct and reconstitute the last traces of the Romantic image of the poet. This is a difficult book to absorb or even summarise. O'Hara is fascinated with the Nietzschean concept of tragic knowledge, and he does attempt to ground it in history, but, by comparison with the sophistication of his critical apparatus, his historical grasp is weak and uncertain. He claims, for example, that Lady Gregory helped Yeats to 'simplify his confused mind by having him collect folk tales from her peasants – the basis for *The Celtic Twilight*'; but 'peasants' had long since disappeared from the Irish countryside, and the first edition of *CT* was published some three years before he even met Lady Gregory. O'Hara accuses J.B. Yeats of being an 'irresponsible landowner', but what was a responsible one in the 1880s if not someone like J.B. Yeats who transferred his land to his tenants and surrendered all claims to inherited wealth? Perhaps most revealing are O'Hara's comments on the last sentence of *R*, which contain the phrase about life being 'a preparation for something that never happens': 'It deserves the attention it has gotten...primarily because it suggests that in 1914-15 Yeats feels a deep dissatisfaction with his life, and, by implication, with his artistic rendering of that life'. But the concluding sentence of *R* appears in Yeats' journal entry for September 1909 (see *Memoirs*, p. 230). So when was Yeats feeling dissatisfied – in 1914-15, in 1909 or in all these years? We need to know, for the answer materially affects the force of O'Hara's argument. Ironically, if he had attended to the social and historical contexts of Yeats' autobiography, he might have revealed more sharply the workings of tragic knowledge, for the middle Yeats was only too aware of history moving against him.

Lipking's is an original inquiry (1981) into the beginning and ending of poetic careers. Accepting the testimony of poems as decisive evidence about how poets conceive or invent their careers, he examines three biographical moments that get into poems, namely initiation, summing up and passage beyond the grave. A poet who wishes to grow 'must learn to read his own early work', and in the light of this remark Lipking juxtaposes Dante's *La Vita Nuova*, Blake's *Marriage of Heaven and Hell*, and Yeats' *PASL*, all three being about how poets read their works. Lipking maintains that the question that haunts *PASL* is whether or not Yeats' poetic career can be renewed. According to Lipking, Yeats renews himself not by completing his initiation but by recapturing his sense that it is about to begin. Thus every paragraph of *PASL* contains material for new poems, and becomes a blueprint for initiation. As to the final moment – the 'tombeau' – Lipking insightfully compares Auden's 'In Memory of W.B. Yeats' with 'Under Ben Bulben', where Yeats enjoys picturing himself dead. Auden, utterly un-Yeatsian in his commemoration of Yeats, yet reveals in the last section Yeats' voice, and in this way, Yeats teaches Auden how to praise: the constant theme, that is, of *LP*.

Finally, the student might find it useful to refer to critical essays on the general theory of autobiography in Olney (1980a). Though not specifically about Yeats, the two essays by Olney on 'Autobiography and the Cultural Moment: A Thematic, Historical, and Bibliographical Introduction' and on 'Some Versions of Memory/Some Versions of Bios: The Ontology of Autobiography', together with Gusdorf's 1956 essay, 'Conditions and Limits of Autobiography', provide a valuable framework for exploring Yeats and autobiography. Gusdorf in particular illuminates everything he touches. The preoccupation with autobiography, he tells us, is not a universal concern but emerges when myths give way to history, when it is seen as valuable to fix one's own image, when a curiosity about the self and destiny develops. Biography and history are external; autobiography implies a new spiritual revolution, where the writing subject reconstitutes him/herself in the focus of his/her special unity and identity across time. Autobiographies sometimes involve the idea of a privileged witness, posthumous propaganda, or alternatively they can enact 'a revenge on history'. Sometimes they assume the task of reconstructing the unity of life through time, allowing a 'second reading of experience'. They are beyond truth or falsity, there to create and, in creating, to be created. The relevance of this essay to *A* and especially to *R* makes itself felt throughout, and Gusdorf could have been writing about Yeats when he says, 'He wrestles with his shadow, certain only of never laying hold of it'.

A Vision and the Occult

Yeats' occult activities

Most readers have to brace themselves before tackling Yeats' most complex prose work, *AV*. But before they do so, students might well explore Yeats' involvement in ceremonial magic and other occult practices, as well as consider *PASL*, the prose work that immediately precedes *AV*. To understand Yeats and the occult properly, we should resist the rush to judgment, noting on the one hand Yeats' remark that 'the mystical life is the centre of all that I do and all that I think and all that I write' (*L*, p. 211), and on the other hand MacNeice's wry comment that 'there was always a sceptic in Yeats', for, ironically, the more we know about this subject the less 'occult' it becomes.

Harper (1974) traces Yeats' involvement in the Order of the Golden Dawn, especially during the period 1896 to 1902, the years which spanned the writing of *SB*. For a more detailed history of the Order itself, see Howe (1972). Yeats was initiated into the Order on 7 March 1890, and by the end of that year the Isis-Urania Temple numbered some 50 people, including Florence Farr Emery, Annie Horniman and Moina Bergson, the French philosopher's sister who was married to MacGregor Mathers and to whom Yeats later dedicated *AVA*. It was a new Order in need of rituals, organisation and control, but Mathers, from his base in Paris, attempted to gain total control of the London Temple and in 1896 sent a manifesto to senior members demanding complete submission: this was resisted. Yeats continued to respect Mathers and visited him in Paris in April 1898 for help in composing the rituals for the Castle of the Heroes, but by 1899 his attitude had cooled. Harper outlines the history of the split in the Order in 1900, Mathers' abortive effort through Aleister Crowley to seize the London headquarters (what Howe calls 'the battle of Blythe Road'), and Mathers' later expulsion. In April 1900 Yeats was elected Imperator of the Outer Order's Isis-Urania Temple by the New Executive and became responsible for instruction in Mystical Philosophy. But he remained troubled by the reorganisation and by Mathers' expulsion, and the period from April 1900 to February 1901 was one of the unhappiest of his life. There was friction between Farr and Horniman on the new Executive Council over the issue of Secret Groups, and Yeats was forced to take sides. 'Always the advocate of order, peace, and unity', as Harper tells us, Yeats argued that such groups create suspicion among those outside. At a General Meeting on 26 February 1901, Yeats lost the argument and resigned as Imperator. After his defeat Yeats wrote an essay, 'Is the Order of R.R. and A.C. to remain a Magical order?'. In his summary of its contents, Harper comments on Yeats' insistence on the Christian foundation of the Order, his advocacy of a system and discipline, and his conviction that it should be a Magical Order, not a society for experiment and research. After 1902, Yeats became less involved in the Order; nevertheless, he continued to advance through the various levels of adeptship. The Order continued to fragment, especially as a result of the Horos rape trial in 1901-2. In February 1903, Miss Horniman resigned and switched her financial support to the Irish dramatic movement. It was probably in 1914 that George joined the Stella Matutina Temple in London, and after their marriage she and Yeats remained active members of Amoun, the Mother Temple. Even though he resigned from the Order in 1922, Yeats never lost his commitment to its cosmic faith.

Yeats' involvement in the Order of the Golden Dawn has still not been fully addressed in Yeats studies. The publication of *SB* will help, as will the paperback edition of Harper (1974), but there is still much to investigate. In a letter to Miss Horniman, dated 8 January 1896, Mathers writes: 'Do not forget that the words "person", "personality" are derived from the Latin word "Persona" which means "a mask" '. This is many years before Yeats began formulating his distinction between character and personality or outlining his Doctrine of the Mask. It may be that Yeats' ideas here owe more to Mathers than previously allowed. Drama and the occult is another subject for further research, not only in terms of rituals and masks, but also in terms of the individuals who mixed in both circles in the 1890s and early 1900s, such as Farr, Horniman, Maud Gonne, John Todhunter and Yeats himself. It is also interesting to note that by the early 1920s, Yeats and a Miss Kate Moffat were the sole surviving members of the Order from its heyday in the 1890s, a fact which sheds additional light on Yeats' idea of 'The Tragic Generation'.

In another book utilising their correspondence between 1896 and 1918, Harper (1980) traces Yeats' relationship with a fellow-occultist, W.T. Horton. The differences between Yeats and Horton in their ideas about art and mysticism help define more closely Yeats' own position. Yeats berates Horton for being too mystical and for not understanding the relationship between art, mysticism and ordinary life: 'Like most visionary and imaginative artists your difficulty is to force yourself to study not the visionary truth but the forms and methods by which it has to be expressed in this world'. Horton tells Yeats that 'all this Spiritism & Spiritistic investigation leads to nothing...arise and leave all these lower things'; his automatic writing sessions with George are 'unreliable, foolish or dangerous'; such activity 'robs the Creative artist of all

& makes him of non-avail & instead of increasing in wisdom like Goethe he becomes vague & incomprehensible like Blake in his prophetic books'. Seen from this perspective, Yeats not only had to contend with competing demands of being an Adept and an Artist, but also had to steer a difficult path between an interest in automatic writing and a commitment to a mid-position on the Cabalistic Tree of Life.

Other studies exploring Yeats' occult activities and friendships can be mentioned here. In a suggestive essay, Goldman (1976) examines Yeats' interest in mediumship, comments on Leo Africanus' first appearance in a seance given by Mrs Wriedt, and briefly discusses the presence of mediums in his poems. Other essays in Harper (1976) consider Yeats' investigation in May 1914 of the so-called miracle of the bleeding oleographs of the Sacred Heart at Mirebeau, his examination in 1912 of the automatic script of a young English girl Elizabeth Radcliffe, the figure of Lionel Johnson as a source for Owen Aherne and Yeats' relationship with Mathers. Yeats' friendship with George Russell (AE) is charted in Kuch's full-length study (1986), which includes a valuable discussion of the differences between the mage and the mystic, between Yeats' ambition as mage to communicate with the spirits and AE's more mystical belief in the act of vision, in seeing the spirits as astral light. AE is the subject of Yeats' story 'An Irish Visionary' in *CT*, and he is also, according to Kuch, the narrator in 'Rosa Alchemica'. If so, the story can then be read as an implicit critique of AE's view that a return to the pagan gods would not meet with strong resistance from the Catholic country people.

Per Amica Silentia Lunae

PASL (1918), which contains an extensive meditation on the Doctrine of the Mask, looks back to the 1890s occult stories such as 'Rosa Alchemica' and forward to the 1920s philosophical discourse of *AV*. Levine (1983), taking up Bloom's suggestion that the period between late-1915 and late-1917 was the most important in Yeats' imaginative life, provides a full-scale commentary on *PASL*. Levine claims that *PASL* should not be seen as an ur-text of *AV* but rather as pivotal, for in this way 'we can learn to find in his pattern of daimonic renewal the visionary centre of his art'. Ch. 1 – in some respects Levine's finest – traces the evolution of the idea of the Mask in the decade before *PASL*, how the debate between the self and the anti-self was central to Yeats' career, and how *PASL* and 'Ego Dominus Tuus' marked a major turning-point. Among his observations we can notice the following: as early as 1886 Yeats was writing about a second self (see *VE*, p. 735), so this did not begin with his journal entries in 1908-9; whereas Wilde used a mask as a form of lying, the Occult Mask was a way of confronting the hidden truth; Dante's *Vita Nuova* helped Yeats see how perhaps he too had lost his way in the middle of life and how the image of the anti-self 'may be an unearthly presence that singles out the poet for guidance'; the episode in July 1915 when Leo Africanus claimed to be the poet's guide gave Yeats 'a means of transforming the mind's internal doubts into a debate with an external anti-self'; after 'Ego Dominus Tuus' Yeats stopped worshipping the Mask and began 'assuming it for what he could learn from it'. This chapter is full of perceptive discriminations and provides the groundwork for the more detailed discussion of *PASL* which follows.

In outlining the development of the argument in *PASL* through the various sections, Levine comments on the origin of the word 'daimon', compares and contrasts 'Anima Hominis' and 'Anima Mundi', and insists on the poetic and not the occult underpinnings of the work. In other chapters on drama and poetry, he stresses the autobiographical imprint in the plays written between 1916 and 1924, while in his discussion of the poetry between 1910 and 1921 he emphasises the value of *PASL* in enabling Yeats to work through 'his creative quarrels with himself'. Comparing the two versions of 'The Wild Swans at Coole', printed in the 1917 Cuala edition and the 1919 Macmillan edition, he comments on the way Yeats liberated himself from the burden of the past, particularly in regard to Maud Gonne, and how the love poems of 1918-19 exhibit a 'new affectionate freedom'. A final chapter on reading Yeats without *AV* argues for the priority of *PASL*, for in *AV* Yeats moves 'farther away from his imaginative vision of himself and of his necessary poetic opposites'. Further discussion of *PASL* can be found in Bloom (1970), as well as Langbaum (1977) and Lipking (1981).

A Vision

Between 20 October 1917 and 28 March 1920 Yeats and his wife spent part of nearly every day on automatic writing, filling over 3600 pages in 450 sittings. In a fascinating study of this material, Harper

(1987) delineates the immediate context for understanding *AV*. He begins by reconstructing their regular sessions. They sat at a table, normally at night, with the lights on. They were alone, no observers being permitted. It seems that George did not go into a trance, and in the early period (5-20 November 1917) and again at the end (16 June 1919-March 29 1920) she jotted down both questions and answers, a 'method that does not suggest full automatism'. To what extent they tried to pattern their experiments on the traditional seance is not clear, but on one occasion there is a reference to the 'glass globe' or crystal ball. George always maintained that she was only a Medium or Interpreter for the Controls or Guides, who were responsible for many of the 'factual' details in *AV*, such as the 'Table of the Four Faculties' (*AVA*, pp. 30-3). Yeats soon became convinced that the Communicators 'had come to excite his creative imagination at a time when the well of inspiration was drying up'.

In their early sessions, during their honeymoon in 1917, Yeats was still suffering from a sense of betrayal towards Iseult Gonne, to whom he had proposed earlier that summer. He was also keen to pursue with the Communicators the nature of his relationship with Maud Gonne and what might have attracted him to all three women, but George – understandably – sought to avoid the personal. This was also the period when *The Only Jealousy of Emer* was gestating, and Yeats questions the Control over the use and significance of the withered arm in the play. As to the Communicators, we learn that Leo is a Frustrator, that Marcus is not a very good Control and that Thomas of Dorlowicz shows concern for Yeats' well-being. It is Thomas who tells him to drink more and take more exercise and the same prosaic Control who informs him – this is, given the context, highly amusing – that it is 'no use having a theory if it tires you'. While at Stone Cottage between 8 and 12 November, Yeats was concerned with two questions: the relation between the Anima Mundi and the Antithetical Self, and the quality in the Anima Mundi that compels that relationship. The Control, countering the tendency in Yeats to assign a higher value to the Antithetical Self and to the unconscious, sensibly insists on the need for balance between the Daily and the Antithetical Self. There also emerges from this account the human side of Yeats, a middle-aged man torn between three women, anxious about his choice of marriage partner and impossibly deluded in his conviction, according to Harper, that he and George had been 'selected to give birth to the New Master or Avatar of the historical cycle soon to begin', a delusion, we might add, that can also colour our reading of 'The Second Coming'.

The next step along the compositional path towards *AV* can be found in the introduction to *AVA* by Harper and Hood (1978). This begins with a discussion of the origins of *AVA* in a 1914 cross-correspondence between something a Control said to Lady Lyttelton and Horton's 'scrap of paper concerning chariot with black & white horses'. The Control indicated that 'Yeats is a prince with an evil counsellor', while Horton had warned the poet about the dark horse driving his chariot into the enemy's camp. Black and white winged horses feature again in one of the earliest sessions of George's automatic writing and again in a Sleep of 11 January 1921. Yeats was so impressed by the original cross-correspondence that, according to the editors, 'Horton's prophetic warning is central to *AV*'. In March 1920 Yeats and George adopted a new method of experimentation, whereby George spoke while asleep. From this date until March 1924 the number of such sessions totalled 164, which, together with the 450 automatic writing sessions conducted between October 1917 and June 1921, constitutes the seven-year quest for visionary truth, during which time *AVA* was composed. The editors discuss the MS content and organisation of the Card File. They track the relationship between the automatic script, the Card File, and *AVA*, and provide detailed evidence of the process of composition. They also comment on the difficulty Yeats had in completing the book, the restructuring of Book IV, and the dedication to Moina Mathers. To complete this thorough edition there are 83 pages of notes, a bibliography which includes books on which Yeats relied in writing *AVA* (see also O'Shea, 1985), and an index to the text itself.

A summary of the contents of *AVA*, as well as a comparison between the 1925 and the 1937 editions, can be found in Peterson (1982) and Archibald (1983). *AVA* contains four major essays: 'What the Caliph Partly Learned', 'What the Caliph Refused to Learn', 'Dove or Swan', and 'The Gates of Pluto'. *AVB* contains five books: Book I follows closely the first essay in *AVA*; Book II is an entirely new essay; Book III is a rewriting of 'The Gates of Pluto'; Book IV is an expansion of 'What the Caliph Refused to Learn'; and Book V, 'Dove or Swan', remains unchanged. Hough (1984) comments on the differences between the two editions, notes that 130 out of 250 pages of *AVA* reappear unaltered in *AVB*, and that Yeats improved the geometrical material relating to cones and gyres and to the Great Year. According to Hough, 'everything of substance in *A* is either reproduced identically in *B* or is present in an amended form'. Fortunately, the two chapters that have provoked most discussion – 'The Great Wheel' and 'Dove or Swan' – are substantially the same in both editions.

Henn's summary (1950) of the contents of *AV*, containing several of the diagrams from the text as well as his own sketch of The Gyre, is still very valuable. Stock (1964), who devotes one chapter to a summary and one to comment, is also helpful. For Stock, *AV* increased Yeats' power as a poet; after composing it his thought moved with new swiftness and precision. Ellmann (1948), in his chapter 'Esoteric Yeatsism', outlines the presence of the System in the poetry written after 1917, notices how the prophetic authority of 'The Second Coming' stems from *AV*, and suggests that the poetry is *AV*'s justification. This line of discussion, which takes its bearings from the Control who told Yeats that they had come 'to give you metaphors for poetry' (*AVB*, p. 8), is perhaps the predominant one among the critics. Rajan (1965) tells us that *AV* is best approached as a group of interrelated symbols, which 'needs to be imaginatively rather than literally received'. Closely linked is the question of how much we need to know of the System to understand the poetry. For Rajan, 'it is to the poetry that we should direct ourselves, and though esoteric interpretation is sometimes helpful and at other times necessary, it has to be controlled by a firm sense of the poem'. Some critics move uneasily between Yeats' occult practices and his poetry, and make little use of *AV*. In a study which seems uncertain both in its aims and organisation, Flannery (1977) discusses Yeats as magician; the connection between magic, poetry, sex and Ireland; the influence of Blavatsky, Chaterjee and others on Yeats and the idea of the Celtic twilight. In a final chapter she argues vigorously for 1912 being the date of composition for 'Ego Dominus Tuus' – though where all this leads to is an open question. Young (1975), too, lacks an overall perspective and begins inauspiciously with some over-general remarks on magic, Shakespeare and the nature of poetry. He claims that by 1914 Yeats knew it was impossible to revive the primitive magic of Irish bards, but thought certain forms of word magic were still possible. This leads Young into a discussion on Symbolism and into the speculation that Yeats' ultimate aim is exorcism.

For students wishing to deepen their understanding of *AV*, both in itself and in how it relates to Yeats' work generally, it is worth referring to Moore (1954), Vendler (1963), Whitaker (1964), Frye (1965), Bloom (1970), Olney (1980), Hough (1984) and Raine (1986). In the last poem Yeats wrote – 'The Black Tower' – there is a reference to 'oath-bound men'. Moore interprets this as a 'warning to critics that a fund of material which might help explain his life and views must remain secret'. Since she wrote her study, that material has become for the most part available, so that some of her comments – such as the assumption that Yeats' spiritistic investigations occupied only five years between 1911 and 1916 ('Mrs Yeats agrees with this estimate') have to be treated with caution. Moore's remarks on *AV* belong to a wider discussion, outlining the development of Yeats' esoteric beliefs from their origins in childhood, Irish lore and Druidism, Blake and Hermetism, through the Golden Dawn, to *AV* and the renewed interest in philosophy after 1920. One of her last chapters explores the question 'Was Yeats a Christian?'. Specifically on *AV* Moore looks at the 'system as a thing in itself', and finds Yeats' attribution of people to different phases 'incredible'. Yeats' method, she believes, is 'emotional rather than logical', and the Four Faculties are muddled, the Mask and Creative Mind tending to run together. Moore also comments on the changes to *AV* and, unlike other critics, descries in *AVB* 'a new book'. She notices, for example, the switch in emphasis from the antithetical Robartes to the primary Aherne, the increased clarity in argument and presentation, new insights into the relation between the Four Faculties and the Four Principles, and that the Daimon is no longer a being exterior to a person but the latter's permanent being, the Ghostly Self. Between the two editions Yeats had benefitted from his reading in philosophy. Plotinus showed him that each person has one of Plato's Divine Ideas; Cusanus that the form of knowing above the antinomies can be a kind of not-knowing; Berkeley that consciousness is all; McTaggart 'the mystery of the whole being active in every part, and the bliss of immortal selves contemplating other selves'; and Gentile that we have 'a foretaste of eternity in our very cognition'. It is this chapter on 'Philosophy as Weapon' that is particularly fine. It can be supplemented by Yeats' correspondence with Sturge Moore (Yeats, 1953), which contains among other things the celebrated discourse on Ruskin's cat, Yeats' attacks on the philosophical position of G.E. Moore, Bertrand Russell and Croce, as well as Sturge Moore's objection to the final stanza of 'Sailing to Byzantium', an objection that in turn spurred Yeats into writing 'Byzantium'.

Virginia Moore's investigations showed what was possible if critics were open to the challenge of Yeats' thought, and subsequent inquiries invariably acknowledge their debt to her pioneering work. Vendler, in a book referred to in the discussion of last plays (1963), provides an outline of each of the five Books of *AVB*. In her chapter on 'The Great Wheel' she suggests that the Four Faculties are different ways of looking at the world and that the Daimon is often symbolised by Yeats in the image of sexual intercourse, so that the Daimon is in part Yeats' 'barbaric recasting of the image of the Muse'. All this is by way of introduction to her central thesis, which relates *AV* to aesthetic and not esoteric doctrine. Each of the five Books of *AV* centres on literature and the imagination: I on literary history, II on poetic creation, III on poetic activity, IV on the imaginative shaping of history, and V on the Muse. In her discussion of Books II and III Vendler makes effective use of Blake's poem 'The Mental Traveller', which she interprets in terms of the imagination and the transmutation of experience. In reference to Byzantium she identifies the discontinuous pattern which allows for perpetual recurrence – thus Byzantium is both the glory of a Christian civilisation and the manifestation of a dying classicism. 'The Soul in Judgment' Vendler interprets as being 'essentially concerned with the aesthetic process as it occurs in the creating mind'. 'Dove or Swan' deals with the passage of the imagination from its classical antithetical phase, where the Swan is Jove the Impregnator, to its single-minded Christian phase, where the Dove is the Holy Ghost, and it provides, therefore, a commentary on 'Leda and the Swan', in which Leda is identified with Yeats. As history, Book V is either nonsense or guesswork, but this further supports Vendler's argument that the Phases act as symbolic commentaries on experience. In her conclusion she suggests that the primary question of *AV*, which is taken up by the plays, is 'how do we account for the perpetual vigour of the imagination, and how should we react in the presence of an obsolete poetic tradition?'.

AV, as Moore, Vendler and Harper (1987) remind us, stands somewhere between philosophy, aesthetics and the occult. Again, we might notice how Yeats crosses demarcation lines between categories and genres: even in a complex prose work explaining his System, he finds a place for poems such as 'The Phases of the Moon' and 'All Souls' Night' and for a story about Michael Robartes. Whitaker (1964) explores Yeats' subjective dialogue with history and discerns two basic attitudes: creative vision and dramatic experience. Under the heading of history as vision, Whitaker reflects on the provenance of cycles in Yeats' early work and on his lifelong search for unity with cosmic forces, a search which after 1896 took an apocalyptic turn. He also discerns a threefold shift in Yeats' view of history between 1889 and 1919: Yeats first sees history as contradictory, then in the 1900s as an artistic and social ideal (he had been reading Castiglione), and after 1910 he tends to vacillate between opposites in a search for a single aspect which would combine a personal with a universal history. For our purposes, the central chapter is a discussion of 'Dove or Swan', which, according to Whitaker, sets forth the panorama of Western history, and which also provides the intermediate stage between the raw data of history and the dense symbolism of his poetry. 'Dove or Swan' is a vision of history as art, an attempt to 'hold in a single thought reality and justice' (*AVB*, p. 25), a 'coherent reverie', 'God's eye view of history'. If taken literally or finally it is deterministic, but 'Dove or Swan', Whitaker claims, is a romantic, subjective vision dramatising 'Yeats' central belief that acceptance of history is at one with freedom and creativity'.

In the second half of his study, Whitaker explores what he takes to be the complementary idea of history as dramatic experience. Under this heading, Yeats had to acquire not just historical knowledge but self-knowledge, and he also had to learn through autobiographical poetry, through passion and detachment and through tragic joy, how to transcend history, to 'merge the active voice of social criticism with the contemplative voice of self-purgation'. Yeats turned to his family heritage to establish a possessive relation to Ireland but was conscious of his family as both community and loss. As the poet of Anglo-Ireland in the

1920s, with his symbol a Tower grounded in the soil of Anglo-Ireland, Yeats moved from Ireland and personal experience to a universal history and eventually came to merge history as dramatic experience with history as panoramic vision. This combination of two views of history is traced by Whitaker in his chapters 'Resurected Gods' and 'Buried Men'. In 'Resurrected Gods' he compares the apocalyptic sensibility of 'Nineteen Hundred and Nineteen' with the assertion of the power of the intellect over destructive forces in 'The Statues'; in 'Buried Men' he explores, as part of the final music of Yeats' dialogue with history, the poet's retrospective glance at historical figures such as Parnell and Casement. Whitaker closes with Yeats' remark to Dorothy Wellesley in May 1937, which justifies the direction of his whole study: 'I begin to see things double – doubled in history, world history, personal history' (Yeats 1940, p. 135). Whitaker's thesis has been very influential in Yeats criticism, but I would have preferred to see a more critical, less 'synthetic' approach, one that analysed Yeats' panoramic view of history or Anglo-Ireland, and that attended to the historical contexts within which Yeats' dialogue with history took place.

Yeats' view of history as contained in *AV* is pursued in Frye (1965), a thoughtful, condensed essay that, broadly summarised, focuses on the relationship between a cyclical and a dialectical view of history. Frye suggests that while both views are present in Yeats' poetry, only the cyclical one is there in *AV*, which leads him to conclude that the poetry is closer to his thought than *AV*. Of his three sections, the first outlines Yeats' cosmology against the background of Western thought, and explores the way analogy and identity (A is like B; A is B) underlie both simile and metaphor and also the two major patterns of poetic imagery, the cyclical and the dialectical. According to Frye, the central principle of symbolism is the analogy between the human and the natural world. He distinguishes cyclical or rebirth symbolism, which stresses the social and historical rather than the individual, and dialectical symbolism, which divides reality into the apocalyptic and the demonic, where all images are identified by metaphor. The dialectical structure of symbolism is clear in the poetry but not in *AV*. Frye's second section examines the historical cycle of symbolism, lists the differences in *AV* between the primary and the antithetical, takes Yeats to task for his unbalanced, traditionalist, neo-pagan treatment of the theme of contemporary annunciation, and suggests that Yeats' cycle concerns not so much human life as human imagination. In the third section, Frye considers the Four Faculties, the concept of Dreaming Back, and Yeats' preference for cyclical as opposed to dialectical symbolism. He contrasts *AV* with the poetry and finds that there is nothing in *AV* to correspond to a poem such as 'Sailing to Byzantium' where the presence of both the eternal and the apocalyptic complicates the single view. The key to Yeats' thought lies not in *AV* but in his poetry: what poems such as 'News From the Delphic Oracle' and 'Byzantium' reveal is that the image is a product of the imagination and that 'the process of redemption is to be finally understood as an identification with Man and a detachment from the cyclical image he has created'.

In other books and studies Frye reflects on the implications of Yeats' theory of history. He discusses (1976a) Yeats' notion that two contrasting types of civilisation have dominated the Western world in turn: classical culture (conceived as heroic, aristocratic and violent, and whose central myth is Oedipus) and Christian culture (democratic and altruistic, whose central myth is Christ). At the beginning of both cultures there stands the conjunction of a woman and a bird – Leda and the Swan and the Virgin and the Dove respectively. Tragedy lies at the heart of classical culture, comedy at the heart of Christian culture, and after our present culture there will be a return to the classical one. Frye disputes this interpretation of history and argues that the Leda and the Swan cycle was not destroyed by Christianity but survived intact, that the same tragic structures and comic formulas are present in Shakespeare and Dickens, and that the Dove and Swan cycle is not so much an antithesis of its predecessor as an expanded world, though he is perhaps forgetting 'The Shepherd and the Goatherd'. The imaginative universes of romance and Christianity are connected, but they are not the same: 'the myth of Christianity is also a divine comedy which contains a tragedy, and thinks of that tragedy as an episode within a larger comic structure'. The contrast, therefore, between the Oedipal and the Christian myths is, as Frye says in another study (1982), 'a red herring'. Frye concludes with an open denunciation of Yeats' position: 'in our day every genuine issue, in the arts as outside them, is connected with getting clear of all such notions of cyclical historical fatality'.

Bloom (1970), whose comparison between Yeats and Blake was referred to in ch. 2 above, calls *AV* 'a considerable flawed major poem', a 'failure in vision', and suggests that the time to question *AV* is at the start. Bloom accuses Yeats of ignoring Blake's warning that seeking to become more than human we become less so, and suggests that in *AV* Yeats is close to a 'calculated anti-humanism'. He then proceeds to attack Yeats' irrationalism and his flirtation with fascism. *PASL* has a balance that *AV* doesn't have, for in *AV* conflict is seen only in terms of antithetical man and not as also concerned with primary forces. Whereas Blake's vision 'implies the dialectical necessity of choice...Yeats makes explicit a cyclic necessity, which he implies the imagination must accept'. Bloom's other chapter on *AV* provides a less heated account of Books II, III and V.

Olney (1980) concentrates on a strand in the history and psychology of Western thought that unites the Pre-Socratics with Yeats and Jung. Even though Jung never read *AV*, there is 'an astonishing agreement' on a range of concepts, doctrines and beliefs; for example, Jung's collective unconscious and Yeats' Anima Mundi, personal unconscious and Anima Hominis, archetypes, Jung's individuation and Yeats' Unity of Being, synchronicity and minds flowing into each other, cycles of history, shadow figures and masks, the relation of the living to the dead, the daimon and concepts of symbolism, as well as the symbolic significance of their towers, Jung's at Bollingen and Yeats' at Ballylee. Olney eschews these surface similarities and concentrates instead on an approach that links both men with the Platonic tradition. Thus, most of his book is devoted to an outline of Pre-Socratic and Platonic philosophy and its reflection in Western thought, whether in Yeatsian poetics or Jungian psychology, in aesthetics, philosophy or the symbolic mode, or time and history. His chapter 'The Poetics of Mummy Wheat' is concerned with Yeats. For Olney, Yeats' poetry constitutes 'an expression of ancient truths revealed to him by spirits of the past and spirits of the unconscious'; his poetics are 'determined by concepts that are Pythagorean, Heraclitean, Parmenidian, Empedoclean and Platonic'. Yeats' philosophy is rooted in Platonism and his work reflects the Pre-Socratic dilemma of Being and Becoming. Thus, to take some examples, Yeats was always too conscious as a man and too devoted to his craft as a poet, ever to abandon himself to the flow of images from the unconscious; he was always too interested in controversy and in the relation between himself and visionary figures to settle for the security of Being. He was too preoccupied with the need to establish a poise between a natural world of becoming and a supernatural world of being and he recognised that creation was a circular affair: while the poet's creation may imitate God's, God's creation must wait on the poet's. The typical psychological and philosophical progress of a Yeats poem – Olney cites the opening and the closing lines of 'Easter 1916' – is from ego to *eidos* (the ideal archetype of a person or 'new species of man'); it proceeds by way of *logos* and *mythos* and passes from this temporal world to the eternal world of art through the exercise of memory and anamnesis. In terms of rhythm, as in such poems as 'The Circus Animals' Desertion', 'Lapis Lazuli', 'Among School Children', which capture the paradigm of the Yeatsian poetic progress, there is a movement from the casual to the incantational. Students of Yeats must come to their own conclusions about 'the poetics of mummy wheat'. Suffice it to say, the pattern Olney detects resembles what other Yeats critics have identified, although they use a vocabulary and interpretative framework that seems less abstract and intimidating.

In a study addressed to a general literary audience rather than to the professed Yeatsian and which is characterised throughout by good sense, Hough (1984) begins by questioning the idea of an occult 'tradition', as propounded, for example, by Wilson (1958 and 1960). He posits instead a 'family of doctrines and symbolic teachings'; there exists, Hough maintains, a 'kinship between the mystery religions of the ancient world and the modern revival of occultism'. But, paradoxically, while the specific claim of modern occultists to ancient authority is 'dubious, mistaken, or simply false', the underlying claim to ancient lineage is 'true, and even demonstrably true'. Hough also discusses the influence of Blavatsky, the ceremonial magic of the Golden Dawn, the Tree of Life which 'stands clear of all inferior material', and Yeats' interest in mediumship. On *AV*, Hough maintains that it is 'not a dictated text' but an 'artefact'; neither is it a sourcebook for the later poetry, being itself 'poetry'. *AV* belongs to the same genre as the visions of Daniel and Ezekiel, Boehme's *Aurora*, Blake's *The Marriage of Heaven and Hell*, Nietzsche's *Thus Spake Zarathustra*, and has for its central symbol the Great Wheel. Its function in Yeats' thought

– a point stressed by Hough – is to bring together 'his magical speculations and his worldly experience, not in an antinomian marriage of heaven and hell, like Blake's, but a *hieros gamos*, a marriage of heaven and earth in which every feeling or event, from the highest to the lowest, has its own right and its proper place'. As to the relation between the System and the poetry, Hough warns against both the dismissal by Auden and the view of those like F.A.C. Wilson for whom reading *AV* is a 'kind of code-breaking', and claims that it is both 'intricate and indirect'. In a final chapter listing some of the problems and questions that *AV* raises, Hough offers a reply to Bloom: 'Yeats is trying to say that the nature of any individual life depends upon its direction (is it moving towards self-realisation at phase 15, or towards submission to the Other at phase 1?); and upon how far it has travelled between these two poles'. Hough's remarks are invariably judicious, for they stem from a mind that knows instinctively what in the text is sound and what is muddled. In conclusion he notices that *AV* lacks an account of the Beatific vision and sexual love, for Yeats seems more interested in the process between earthly life and the celestial state than in the ultimate goal.

It is appropriate to conclude this chapter with Raine's recent collection of essays (1986), written over a period of 20 years. A characteristic of her style is a certain hectoring pose, as when she claims that 'Yeats' thought was the leading thought of his time'. She is also given to asserting without examining, as when she writes that Yeats passed 'upon the politics of time the judgment of the politics of eternity' – without, incidentally, acknowledging that the phrase comes from AE's *The Interpreters* (1922, p. vii). Raine's first essay 'Hades wrapped in Cloud', first published in Harper (1976), is a rambling affair, in spite of which she covers much of the ground relating to Yeats and the occult. In another essay comparing Yeats and Blake she observes perceptively that the common feature of their thought is neither image nor mythology but 'precisely its diagrammatic character'. An essay on Blake and *AV* examines the diagrams both used, the equivalence between Urizen, Los, Luvah and Tharmas and Yeats' Four Faculties of Creative Mind, Body of Fate, Will and Mask. Raine also draws attention to their differences: in *AV*, quaternity surfaces as polarized opposites; Luvah and Urizen rotate; for Blake, time is a fall from the eternal mode, whereas Yeats sees time in terms of change and the rearrangement of the constant elements in his Zodiac according to the phases; for Blake, human history is a progressive unfolding of a divine plan, whereas Yeats' periodisation is linked to his idea of the 'stylistic arrangements of experience' (*AVB*, p. 25). Among Yeats' specific debts to Blake, Raine notices the way Blake's poem 'The Mental Traveller' is always present when Yeats is thinking of gyres, and how the rocking cradle in 'Jerusalem' seems to be the source for the image in 'The Second Coming'. Other essays deal with Yeats and the Golden Dawn, Yeats' preoccupation not so much with death as with 'that other life', Yeats and Kabir (how the idea of the mortal self juxtaposed with the immortal soul underlies 'Among School Children'), and Yeats and Christianity. In a final essay Raine offers an *apologia pro vita sua* – from positivism as an undergraduate to her later conversion to Catholicism. Through Blake she discovered a weapon against modern scientific materialism as well as the figure of Yeats and his 'contemporary reaffirmation of unageing intellect'.

Chapter 5
Yeats and the Irish Context

Yeats and 19th-Century Ireland

Yeats and the oral tradition

When critics discuss Yeats' lineage they often overlook the Irish oral tradition. But no other modern writer has taken the oral tradition so seriously. In all the variety of its forms and modes of expression – fairy and folktales, heroic myths, ballads and songs; in all that 'the people say to each other on fair-days and high days' (Yeats, 1889, p. vii); in all that the country people believed; in all the settings and situations of that tradition, whether the hedge-school culture of the 18th century, or the cross-roads of rural Ireland where the dancing and singing took place, or that characteristic intimate setting for story-telling 'bent above a sinking fire' (*PNE*, p. 216), or listening to sailors' yarns in Sligo or Howth; in all those childhood years listening to the stories of Mary Battle, stories which would have included the 1798 rebellion and the sighting of the French ships at Killala – in all this, Yeats shows himself highly conversant with and deeply sympathetic towards the Irish oral tradition.

As a child in Sligo he made frequent trips inland to Glencar Waterfall, Lough Gill and the magical Isle of Innisfree; he went fishing out at sea, often very early in the morning; he rode his red pony round the countryside; he climbed mountains. A budding naturalist, he was also surrounded by the oral tradition, by the myths associated with Knocknarea and Ben Bulben and by the stories of fisherfolk at Rosses Point. Between the ages of seven and nine, he lived at Merville, the Pollexfen home in Sligo, and he returned there for holidays from England via the Liverpool-Sligo steamer that belonged to his grandfather. Sligo became imprinted on his soul: it is said that in later life his conversation was constantly punctuated by reference to Sligo and its legends and stories. 'Ireland is always Connacht to my imagination, for there more than elsewhere is the folk tradition that is the loftiest thing that has come down to us within the ring of Ireland' (*Ex*, p. 231). His chief sources of knowledge about folklore were Paddy Flynn of Ballysodare and Mary Battle, his uncle's family servant, whose mind was 'rammed with every sort of old history and strange belief' (*R*, pp. 133-4); indeed, he admitted that 'much of my *Celtic Twilight* is but her daily speech'. But Yeats was caught between Sligo and London, between an oral and a literary tradition. The summer of 1887 he spent in Sligo collecting stories from local people in the area; during the same year he was at the British Museum researching into the Irish stories as they had been written down by his predecessors in the field; especially, Crofton Croker (1824, 1834) and Kennedy (1866, 1870). Fortunately, both activities proved successful, the first leading to *CT* (1893), the second to *Fairy and Folk Tales of Ireland* (1888) and *Irish Fairy Tales* (1892). But, equally, we can detect in the two activities not only the gulf between two traditions, but also Yeats' attempt by various literary means – including writing ballads and stories – to negotiate it. In the 1880s and 1890s he was learning how to become a spokesperson for Irish culture and could not therefore neglect the oral tradition; and always he sought to do more with the given parameters, so that it isn't too fanciful to discern in the character of Hanrahan, the journeyman poet and singer, Yeats' ambition to write himself into the oral tradition.

One of the best introductions to Yeats and the Irish oral tradition can be found in Thuente (1980). She discusses in turn Yeats' debt to his 19th-century predecessors, his folklore anthologies of 1888 and 1892, the movement from fairy to folk in *Representative Irish Tales* (1891) and *CT*, the poets and heroes of *SR*, and what she terms Yeats' 'traditional innovations' in literary theory and style. Thuente distinguishes folklore from mythology: folklore consists of the broad range of oral traditions – narratives, songs, beliefs, customs – that belonged to the country people; mythology refers to the narratives about the ancient gods and heroes. Yeats, she maintains, was involved in the 1880s and 1890s more with folklore than with mythology. As an editor and collector, Yeats passed through 'four successive Irish subjects – fairies, contemporary peasants, 18th-century rogues and raparees, and ancient heroes – and through several genres – folk belief legends, Anglo-Irish fiction, folk hero legends, and ancient myth'. This is a perceptive study with an impressive coverage, where we can read about O'Leary's influence in inspiring Yeats to consider folklore a serious literary subject-matter, the importance of Hyde's collections and translation of Irish oral traditions (Yeats particularly admired Hyde's simple and sincere style) and Yeats' place among other 19th-century collectors of Irish folklore. Part of the problem for the critic is establishing markers, knowing what to include, finding a path between the two traditions. Thuente has made a significant contribution in mapping this out, but more could be done. One small point can serve for many. Thuente claims that Yeats' classification of the fairies 'is based on his distinction between the "trooping" or sociable fairies and the more malignant or "solitary" fairies, and is not found in any of his predecessors in Irish folklore. Croker had not distinguished or mentioned any such distinction'. On the contrary, Croker (1834), as his notes to the section on trooping fairies make clear, was quite aware of the basis on which he made his selection. At issue here – and we need to remember that a quarter of Yeats' 1888 anthology is taken up with material from Croker – is the way Yeats conceals his debt to Croker. Critics should not assume that Yeats is correct when he accuses Croker of failing to 'take the populace seriously' and of imagining the country 'a humorist's Arcadia' (Yeats, 1888, p. xv). For such swerves away from a possible influence – such 'clinamen' in Bloom's terms – always need further investigation.

Other studies can be briefly mentioned. Hirch's essay (1979) provides a short, authoritative survey of Yeats' commitment to Irish folklore and suggests that 'the spectrum of his folklore writings is more considerable than is generally recognised'. Hirch refers to Yeats' 'ill-fitting role of the scientific folklorist', a point that needs more expansive treatment, for Yeats eschewed the increasingly scientific direction of folklore studies as represented, for example, by Alfred Nutt in England, or O'Hanlon (1870) and Curtin (1890) in Ireland. What interested Yeats was the way 19th-century Irish collectors 'made their work literature rather than science, and told us of the Irish peasantry rather than of the primitive religion of mankind, or whatever else the folklorists are on the gad after' (Yeats, 1888, p. xiv). In a full-length study, Kinahan (1988) claims that the primary influences on Yeats' emerging thought were folklore and occultism. Kinahan argues persuasively that Yeats' early work is not escapist and that the revival of interest in Irish folklore and magic encouraged Yeats in his search for unity.

'Yeats' early use of the magical tradition is at its most effective when the private voice of the magus is subsumed by the more public voice of the artist, and at its least effective when the voice of the magus supersedes that of the poet.' Kinahan then discusses the 19th-century interest in the Irish folktale. He writes well about the lamia motif (the grin of malice masked by a face smiling welcome) and how this reappears in a poem such as 'The Stolen Child'. Yeats hesitated to give himself wholly to the supernatural world and eventually opted for a 'world whose workaday sounds sing peace into the breast'. Oisin in *WO* is a 'rejecter of eternities'; the Rose suggests reconciliation but Yeats refused to be pinned down; his early writings are focused on the warmth of the hearth and the sheltering natural world as in the image of the walled garden. In this respect Kinahan extends Albright's view that Yeats 'used Oisin in *WO* to criticise the myth of the poet's search for the immortal' (Albright, 1972). This takes us slightly away from the oral tradition, but it does suggest the potential that an inquiry into Yeats' use of folklore might reveal.

Yeats and the literary tradition

There has been a continuing interest among critics in Yeats' debt to Gaelic, to the Irish literary ballad and to 19th-century Irish poets. MacDonagh (1916) groups Yeats with Mangan and Ferguson as poets of 'the Irish Mode', a mode he identifies in terms of stress and rhythm: Irish verse 'frequently allows for the clear pronunciation of several syllables between stress and stress'. He ascribes the musical quality of Yeats' early verse to 'that Irish chant which at once saves Irish speech from too definite a stress and from an utterance too monotonous and harsh'. The distinctive character of Hiberno-English and its presence in Yeats' work can also be pursued in Power (1967), Meir (1974) and Lucy (1978). With particular reference to the ballads and songs, Meir examines the Anglo-Irish heritage in Yeats' work as a whole, explores the effect of Yeats' abandonment in the 1890s of the ideal of a popular national poetry, and comments on the influence of Hiberno-English on the syntax of his verse. Further discussion of Yeats and Irish folk song can be found in Michael Yeats (1966), which includes a consideration of the originality of 'Down by the Salley Gardens', an examination of the folk songs in Yeats' plays, and some remarks on his father's views on the relationship between music and poetry. According to his son, Yeats 'never achieved his ambition of writing songs which would be sung by "butchers and bakers, and those few persons who sing from delight in words"'.

On Yeats and 19th-century Irish poetry, the student is referred to Kinsella (1970), Brown (1972) and Welch (1980). For Kinsella, 'silence, on the whole, is the real condition of Irish literature in the nineteenth century'. With the death of Gaelic as the language of the Irish people, the modern poet has difficulty making contact with the 18th-century inheritance. 'I stand on one side of a great rift, and can feel the discontinuity in myself.' Yeats created an Anglo-Irish tradition, but actually isolation is the characteristic of his life. Joyce also rejected modern Ireland, but his isolation is 'a mask'. Ironically, 'Yeats stands for the Irish tradition as broken; Joyce stands for it as continuous'. Kinsella's is an important essay not so much for resiting Yeats in the 19th century as for re-evaluating Yeats' place in the 'gapped tradition' that constitutes contemporary Irish culture. Brown, on the other hand, writes more but says less than Kinsella. He is torn between constructing a narrative of events from Thomas Davis in the 1840s to Yeats in the 1890s and simply retelling the known story of Irish politics in these years. His study suffers from being one of the first in the field, for until recently literary critics have had to write their own cultural history of Ireland. It can, however, still be recommended for the occasional insights that pierce the surface narrative. He writes well about the link between 'God Save Ireland', the Fenian popular ballad and Yeats' death mystique; he cautions against the (Yeatsian) view that O'Leary 'belonged to some genteel verbal branch of ethical culture'; and he draws attention to the connection between Yeats, O'Grady and 'Literary Parnellism'. Welch furnishes a more straightforward account of the development of Irish poetry from Moore to Yeats. Until Yeats, 19th-century Irish verse, having no tradition to call its own, lacked 'flexibility', a key word in this study. In his chapter on Yeats, he contrasts the way 'Oisin is the explorer who survives, heroic rage intact, the voyage into the self where Mangan went astray'. Ferguson, on the other hand, possessed an authentic Irish imagination but in the end 'succombed to the deadness around him'. Welch believes that in Oisin, Yeats' surrogate, Yeats gave voice simultaneously to his nationalism and to doubts about his own imaginative structures.

Yeats and 18th-Century Ireland

The place to start an inquiry here is with Torchiana's highly influential study (1966), which examines the flowering of Yeats' interest in Protestant, 18th-century Ireland. Torchiana begins by noticing Yeats' disillusion with 19th-century Ireland, his admiration for Lady Gregory, and how his attraction for 18th-century Protestant Ireland was 'more an attitude or quality of intellect than any necessary class distinction'. Torchiana includes valuable brief sketches of Anglo-Irish figures such as John Shawe-Taylor, Hugh Lane and Robert Gregory. In separate chapters devoted to Swift, Burke, Berkeley and Goldsmith, he comments intelligently on Swift as 'a moral agent for modern Ireland', on Burke's concept of organicism and continuity versus abstraction, on Ruskin's cat and Berkeleyan epistemology, and on Yeats' difficulty in assimilating Goldsmith. In another chapter Torchiana explores the Augustan resonance in Yeats' verse, its elegiac quality, the theme of Anglo-Irish solitude, and the images of *sprezzatura* in *T* and *WS*. The book ends with a fine exposition of *P*, the symbolic tragedy of the 18th century and its consequence for modern Ireland.

Underlying McCormack's challenging study (1985) is Kinsella's 'gapped tradition'. Unlike Torchiana, McCormack takes issue with Yeats' idea of the 18th century. In an interesting move McCormack repositions Yeats within the contradiction between the sociological formation of the Protestant Ascendancy in the 1790s and the later ideological construction elaborated by the poet. According to McCormack, the term 'the Protestant Ascendancy' was first coined in meetings of the Common Council of Dublin Corporation in the 1790s; Yeats – like many others, we might add – used the term to refer to the governing elite in Ireland from the Williamite Settlement of 1697 onwards. There are two aspects to Yeats' concept of tradition; one is an 18th-century hegemony and the other is an Irish literary 'tradition'. For Yeats, the literary 'tradition' is characterised on the one hand by the distinctiveness of the Protestant Ascendancy, and on the other by the absence both of an Irish middle class and of the19th century. Such a tradition is, of course, as McCormack claims, largely a construct by Yeats. In contrast to many critics, McCormack stresses the problematic status of Anglo-Irish literature, contests the view that Anglo-Irish literature is a national literature and insists that only in the work of Yeats and Joyce does a 'coherent Anglo-Irish literature' begin to emerge, in which 'the one body of work opposes or qualifies the other'. But – McCormack quickly adds – it is a coherence ironically based on each denying 'his inherited orthodoxy' and each striving to recreate a 'specifically literary heterodoxy'.

Space permits only two brief observations. Firstly, in stressing the connection between the Protestant Ascendancy and 'tradition', McCormack possibly underestimates Yeats' 19th-century inheritance, and in particular the influence of the oral tradition. Doubtless, McCormack would assign such interest on Yeats' part to his Primitivism, the reverse side of his Augustanism. But Yeats' relationship with an oral tradition is more complex than the term Primitivism will allow. McCormack narrows the discussion about Yeats and tradition to the one that Yeats 'constructed', but the more attention we pay to his relationship with an oral tradition the more we need to go beyond the simple opposition between reflection or construction. Yeats may have been able to 'construct' an 18th-century version of history and call it a tradition, but it is reassuring to know that his relationship with the oral tradition afforded no such easy solutions. Secondly, McCormack assumes that 'tradition' is a 'quintessentially literary concept', standing in contrast with his sociological and historical category of Ascendancy. But if he had pursued a sociological understanding of tradition, he might have been forced to distinguish between 'tradition' and 'traditionalism'. 'Traditionalism' is 'an ideological mode and stance, a mode oriented against the new symbols – making some parts of the older tradition into the only legitimate symbols of the traditional order and upholding them against any "new" trends and innovations' (Eisenstadt, 1973). This seems to me an appropriate characterisation of Yeats' Augustanism. Yeats' 'tradition' is a form of 'traditionalism'. Yeats wanted to impose his understanding of tradition on Irish culture, and to make his traditionalism seem the 'natural' tradition.

Harris (1974), in a study that extends beyond the confines of the 18th century to embrace the Renaissance, concentrates on the changing emphases given to Coole Park and Ballylee in Yeats' work. In his introduction Harris comments on how Yeats' conception of Coole evolved gradually to embrace both aristocratic perfection and responsiveness to public issues, how he typically sought myths of self-explanation and possession, and how he was obsessed with the idea of a numinous place. Ch. 2 focuses on the growing association in Yeats' mind, especially evident in *In the Seven Woods*, between Coole Park and the Renaissance. In a suggestive chapter comparing Coole and Urbino and Yeats and Ben Jonson, Harris discusses Yeats' possible debt to Jonson, the idea of the country house as a reflection of the spiritual and aesthetic values of the inhabitants, and the way the two poets use symbolic detail in the evocation of the country house. The sustained order in Jonson's 'To Penshurst' is contrasted with Yeats' search for meaning from apparently inscrutable images amid a threatening outer world: 'Yeats' country house poems are consequently "about" something quite different from Jonson's: the complex interaction between an individual personality and an ideal, actual world almost lost'. In ch. 4 he examines in more detail the idea of possession. While *R* is 'a myth of dispossession', Thoor Ballylee – 'not an adopted symbol but an ancient image' – represents the felt correlation between house and imagination, the perpetual urge to reconstruct. Harris next notices how Yeats, in poems such as 'The Shepherd and the Goatherd', 'In Memory of Major Robert Gregory', and 'A Prayer for My Daughter', transfers the aristocratic culture from Coole to Ballylee. His concluding three chapters deal with the period from the Civil War to the 1930s and explore Yeats' final attitudes to inherited wealth. Several perceptions stand out. Yeats was impressed by the loss of stamina among the Anglo-Irish (as was O'Grady in the 1880s, we might add); he tightened his imaginative grasp on the Tower by threatening himself with its loss; there is a distinction between the speakers in the poems and the poems themselves; and, finally, Yeats, aware of the demise of the aristocratic tradition, sought in a poem such as 'Coole Park and Ballylee, 1931' to stress the 'cultural continuity' between the two houses.

Yeats and Modern Ireland

Yeats in his own period

For introductory surveys to Yeats in the context of his own period, the student is referred to Boyd (1922), Howarth (1958), Kain (1962), Loftus (1964), Fallis (1977) and Foster (1988). Boyd offers a contemporary impression of the Irish Literary Revival; Howarth deals with a number of Irish writers, including Yeats and AE, who were affected by the rise and fall of Parnell; Kain's is a readable account of Dublin in the age of Yeats and Joyce; Loftus explores the issue of nationalism in modern Irish poetry; Fallis affords a competent, straightforward introduction to the Irish Renaissance; and Foster in his chapter 'The "New" Nationalists' gives a historian's view of Yeats' contemporary context. Students interested in pursuing the theme of Easter 1916 in Yeats' work can begin with Thompson (1967). Compared with AE and O'Casey, who respond respectively with mystical and naturalistic images, Yeats sees the event in tragic terms. As to Yeats' ability to write about history – his 'amazing self-mastery' – Thompson perceptively observes that because Yeats 'lived a myth, history became the myth in which he found himself'. In a more impassioned but less critical inquiry into Easter 1916, Jordan (1987) yokes together Cuchulain, Pearse, the Rose, romantic Ireland and Yeats' 'terrible beauty' in an examination of the Mask and Image and of 'the unbroken continuity and permanence of the Gaelic tradition'. For background information on the participants in the Rising, see the reference section in Malins (1974). For a more advanced survey of Yeats in the 19th century, see the excellent fourth chapter of Marcus (1970). This includes reference to the common ground or otherwise that Yeats enjoyed with Tynan, Hopper, Todhunter, Rolleston, Johnson, AE, Hyde and Larminie. In another well-organised chapter Marcus traces Yeats' involvement in three major literary controversies of the 1890s. These were, firstly, the scheme to publish a popular inexpensive series of Irish books, which brought Yeats into conflict with Duffy and made him aware of the (Young Ireland) inadequacy of treating literature as a political tool; secondly, his dispute with Dowden, which centred on Yeats' insistence that Irish writers should choose Irish subjects and become national rather than cosmopolitan writers; and, thirdly, his differences with the sophisticated cosmopolitanism of John Eglinton (W.K. Magee), who was concerned more with the individual's development towards potential divinity than art, the state, or national literature.

Kenner's recent quirky inquiry (1983) into modern Irish writers considers the central place of Yeats and of writers in his shadow, especially Joyce. With regard to Yeats and Joyce he touches on three main aspects: the biographical influences of one on the other; the parallels between the two writers; the question of their Irishness. Unconventionally, Kenner posits that the middle Yeats was influenced by Joyce. Thus, in 'Easter 1916', Yeats picks up the 'sacerdotal model Stephen Dedalus proposes for art', deRomanises it with his own Yeatsian Magic and 'transfigures the anticlimaxes of Easter 1916 into names for a litany'. On the parallels between Yeats and Joyce, Kenner notices the place of Cuchulain in their work. Joyce's Cuchulain, whom Kenner discerns in the figure of Bloom in the 'Cyclops' episode of *Ulysses*, is not foregrounded as he is in the work of O'Grady and Yeats, but is kept amid 'the clutter of subplots'. Kenner also discerns in Yeats' association of Pearse with Cuchulain, and in Joyce's possible intention in *Finnegans Wake* of waking the corpse of someone executed in the Civil War, an example of the theme of resurrection in their work. He contrasts Yeats' aristocratic fascination with Cuchulain and Joyce's fondness for the more plebeian Finn. As to the relation of Yeats and Joyce to history, while Yeats was withdrawing into the Tower, Joyce was incorporating into *Finnegans Wake* the confusion that beset Irish society in the aftermath of the Civil War. Kenner is less incisive in tackling the third issue of Yeats and Joyce's Irishness; he assumes for example that there is such an unproblematic quality. All facts in Ireland, he tells us, are shrouded in myths, legends and stories: 'any such form of words as "They will tell you in Ireland" means that the next statement, though enlightening, is better not trusted'. Fortunately, Kenner is more alive to the significance of Yeats and Joyce as Irish writers – to the way they appropriated the English language, the English novel and English literary history. For any discussion of the Irishness of Yeats and Joyce has to be understood in 'relational' terms; it has to attend to the hyphen that both separates and joins 'Anglo' and 'Irish'.

Watson (1979) investigates the attempt by Yeats, Joyce, Synge and O'Casey to 'define the nature and meaning of Irish identity'. The value of his study is twofold: in contrast to Kenner, Watson offers a sustained argument about Yeats in the context of other Irish writers, and he also seeks to convert what in history is often seen as background into foreground. In his chapter on Yeats he traces the poet's historical development in terms of the 'anomalous status of the Protestant middle and professional class of Ireland' and how this contributed to his sense of 'not quite belonging anywhere'. Hence Yeats' Anglo-Irish solitude, his commitment to lost causes and his idealisation of the peasantry. The main point of Watson's argument is that the success of the literary movement highlighted the Anglo-Irish predicament, but this led Yeats not to withdraw from public life but to construct two dominant myths: that of the hero, who is conceived as in some way outside of history (for example, 'An Irish Airman Foresees His Death' and 'Easter 1916') and that of the cultured aristocracy, an image made more powerful because of its elegiac quality. Yeats' aesthetic of apocalypse is placed within both an Irish and a European context, but Watson emphasises the Irish cultural situation in Yeats' sense of an ending and the way the poet imbues Anglo-Irish loss with significance.

Ellmann (1970), as his subtitle indicates, seeks to situate 'Yeats among Wilde, Joyce, Pound, Eliot and Auden'. Ellmann's approach is literary rather than cultural, biographical rather than critical. In his chapter on Joyce, he traces the biographical links between the two writers, and emphasises how Joyce absorbed the influence of Yeats. The chief weakness lies in an unwillingness to go beyond biographical connections, to explore, for example, issues focusing on the Irish context of their work, or the deeper critical questions raised by comparisons between their texts. In his conclusion to the Joyce chapter, he writes that 'for Yeats the method of literature was to raise the ordinary to the heroic, for Joyce a movement down was as required as a movement up, and he mingled ordinary, heroic, and mock-heroic without wishing to compound them'. The method is problematic and material which could legitimately form the basis of an inquiry into Yeats and Joyce marks the tantalising end of a chapter. His more recent study (1987), which subsumes Yeats along with Wilde, Joyce and Beckett under the umbrella of Four Dubliners, suffers from a similar reluctance to engage with the critical and cultural interconnections that underlie the separate biographies of this imperial quadrumvirate. Needless to say, there are compensations, not least in Ellmann's remarks about Yeats' Steinach operation in 1934 – which was in fact a vasectomy – and how this 'second puberty' affected his writing in his final years.

Yeats and later Irish writers

The strongest case for the influence of Yeats' drama on later Irish playwrights can be found in Worth (1978). Stressing Yeats' central role in the development of modern drama, Worth sees a direct line from *ATHW* to Beckett's *Waiting for Godot.* Yeats anticipated 'all that is most original in European theatre': the bare, open stage; the symbolist doctrine of the concrete; the dissolving of the frontiers between drama and ballet, and drama and opera; the exploration of the 'interior'; the need to deploy all the resources of the theatre including scene, colour, music, dance and movement. Worth identifies two prominent characteristics in this kind of theatre: one is adventurousness in tackling new subjects, such as solitude – often thought intractable to drama; the other is a commitment to total theatre and the realisation that plays are more than written texts. Worth tracks two particular lines: one from Yeats through O'Casey to the musical drama of John Arden; the other, more inward and unspoken, the drama of the interior, from Yeats to Beckett and Pinter. Her study embraces throughout the European dimension. She begins, for example, with an interesting discussion of Symons and Maeterlinck: Symons provided a guide to the European movement in literature; Maeterlinck offered Yeats 'suggestive models for an interior drama'. In another chapter, 'The Vitality of the Yeatsian Theatre', Worth suggests that today is a favourable time for Yeats' plays to receive their due recognition. A new kind of theatre has begun to emerge – Cocteau's dance plays and the more recent dance dramas of Lindsay Kemp; the musical, rhythmic forms in the work of Craig, Copeau and Artaud; the attack on the dead forms of plot, construction, method in Brook's theatre of cruelty. Writers, too, have been moving in a similar direction, and Yeats, according to Worth, has been, whether consciously or unconsciously, 'a crucial influence' (she instances Masefield, Eliot, Pinter, Auden and Isherwood, and even Edward Bond). This is an important study and should be attended to by those who think that Yeats' drama has no heirs and holds only an oddity value.

The influence of Yeats' poetry on his Irish successors has generated a full-blown discussion, and the student is referred to Kinsella (1970), Lucy (1973), Donoghue (1976), Fallis (1977), Harmon (1979) and Heaney (1980). In a recent survey, Garratt (1986) outlines 'the tradition and continuity from Yeats to Heaney'.

With chapters on Yeats, Joyce, Clarke, Kavanagh, Kinsella, Montague and Heaney, this study covers much of the ground that is often assumed to constitute modern Irish verse. It is a conventional reading. Broadly summarised, it begins with the imposing figure of Yeats and his concept of tradition; Yeats presents problems for the ensuing 'intermediate' generation of Clarke and Kavanagh, and these are followed in turn by the post-war generation of poets, whose work expresses 'the recognition and then the acceptance of a broken literary tradition'. In reaction to Yeats' tradition, and contemporary with him, there is Joyce, who 'tapped the mainstream of modern Irish life, the rising bourgeoisie, and treated it realistically'. Joyce offered to post-Yeatsian poets an alternative to Yeats' heroicising tendency and Ascendancy tradition, for Joyce accepted the divided, fractured tradition and – ironically – bequeathed to the next generation of poets a sense of continuity. There is nothing that is especially new in Garratt's study, and perhaps for this very reason it affords a good starting-place. The more advanced student may want to compare it with Johnston, who traces the line of Irish poetry not back to Yeats but to Joyce (1985).

The issue of continuity and tradition is also discussed in a series of essays on modern Irish literature and society in Deane (1987). Deane observes that Irish literature 'derives from a culture which is neither wholly national nor colonial but a hybrid of both'. Irish writers were obliged to find some way of dealing with history, 'a category which includes language, landscape, and the various ideologies of the recovered past which grew out of them'. The response of the Revival writers to history was 'heroic and astounding', and Yeats, Joyce, Synge and O'Casey were finally enabled by it, producing work which was definitely Irish but which was not limited to that term. After them there was a pause, and it was Kavanagh who deflected the Yeatsian influence by replacing the region of Ireland with the parish. Since the 1960s, however, the pressure of history has returned again. In another essay Deane explores the idea of the Celt in Arnold and Burke. It was Burke, he claims, who in 1792 gave currency to the term 'the protestant ascendency' (sic). In 'The Literary Myths of the Revival' Deane makes a number of useful observations which undermine the conventional view of the Revival: Yeats blurs the distinction between aristocracy and Ascendancy, the latter being, as

McCormack also notices, a predominantly bourgeois formation; the basis for Yeats' idea of Ascendancy is flimsy, predicated on the idea of spiritual loneliness; post-Treaty Ireland put an end to the Revival. In a separate chapter, 'Yeats and the Idea of Revolution' (which according to Said (1988) 'must stand as the most interesting and brilliant account of Yeats' idea of revolution'), Deane explores the way Yeats combined a revolutionary aesthetic with a traditional politics and concludes – perhaps unremarkably – that 'to be a traditionalist in the modern world was to be revolutionary'. These essays, while often stimulating, promise more than they deliver; they contain nothing that has the authority or clinching power of Donoghue (1971), for example, when he remarks that Yeats 'invented a country, calling it Ireland'.

Yeats and Fascism

Yeats and fascism is an issue that has the habit of not going away. Critics who discuss it often write as if they had the final word, sure that Yeats is or is not a fascist or a proto-fascist. Frequently, critics cite a particular passage that they consider puts the matter beyond dispute; for example, Yeats' claim, in reference to events in Europe in 1936, that 'The Second Coming' 'foretold what is happening' (*L*, p. 851). In part the problem takes us back to the question of Yeats' beliefs as already outlined in ch. 2 above, and we need reminding that as a dialectical thinker Yeats can never be easily pinned down. After he turned 60 – and we can see this in his Senate Divorce speech (*The Senate Speeches of W.B. Yeats*, pp. 99 ff.), in the Crazy Jane poems, in 'Under Ben Bulben', as well as in *On the Boiler* (1939) – there is often an outrageous tone in Yeats, as if, knowing that his words no longer carried influence, he could say what he liked. But regardless of the actual content of his remarks, there is something endearing about a public figure who expresses the anger the private citizen often feels about the imperviousness of the State and the seemingly intractable nature of history and society.

The place to begin this inquiry is with O'Brien (1965), who sets out to demonstrate that Yeats' politics are less vague than commonly supposed and that his involvement in politics suggests the poet was not a foolish but a cunning, passionate man. Until 1903 Yeats expressed his Irish side; thereafter, his nationalism became aristocratic and archaizing, and his Protestantism was marshalled against the rising Catholic middle class. Throughout, O'Brien stresses Yeats' calculating nature: he was against the employers during the Dublin Lock-Out of 1913 not for 'humanitarian zeal', as Hone claims, but because the employers represented the Catholic middle class. O'Brien also impugns other motives: Yeats attacked the Church in the Divorce debate not from liberal sympathies but from a superior caste position. His flirtation with fascism dissipated because fascism in Ireland was not likely to succeed; and against those critics who assume that Yeats was a lover of hopeless causes, O'Brien asserts that 'Yeats the man was as near to being Fascist as his situation and the conditions of his own country permitted'. When fissures opened in Irish politics – as in 1891 with the Parnell split, in 1920-2 when Sinn Fein divided, or in 1933 when the Blue Shirts under Duffy emerged – Yeats was tempted into the political arena and wrote with excitement; these 'manic' phases were no less real than the 'depressive' phases which followed. If a collaborationist regime had been established in Dublin, 'one would have expected to see him at least a cautious participant, or ornament'.

The first, and perhaps most effective, rebuttal of O'Brien came with Cosgrave (1967). Cosgrave answers O'Brien point by point. He insists that Yeats was 'all his life an Irish nationalist'; that O'Leary and Yeats shared a mutual insight into the state of Ireland; that O'Brien ignores Yeats' involvement in establishing the Irish literary movement in the 1890s; that there is no authority for assuming that 1902-3 marked Yeats' withdrawal from politics. The 1916 poems reveal not a proto-fascist but a 'terrible conflict and uncertainty in Yeats'. In his discussion of Duffy and the Blue Shirts, O'Brien ignores *AV* and the historical determinism that underlies Yeats' views; equally, Yeats' attitude to what he saw as the coming force 'was far from unambiguously favourable'. According to Cosgrave, O'Brien misreads the last poems, which give no sign of heralding a Fascist Dawn. Yeats had two political attitudes, Cosgrave concludes: 'he was an Irish nationalist and he wanted a government which would provide adequately for what he called "my 'pagan' institutions, the Theatre, the Academy" '.

Cullingford (1981) builds on the work of Cosgrave. In early chapters on O'Leary and Morris, she underlines that O'Leary's nationalism was anti-capitalist, and that Yeats' early socialism 'had a significant and lasting influence upon his later political attitudes'. Morris' legacy can be felt in Yeats' utopianism, his support for the workers in 1913, his advocacy of art galleries and education for the poor, his interest in social legislation embracing the basic necessities for citizens and the need to limit incomes. In another chapter on the Fenians and the Parnellites, Cullingford suggests that *WO* portrays Ireland as being held in chains by England the demon; that the Irish Literary Revival, which emerged after the death of Parnell, was political in inception; and that if Yeats was 'cunning', as O'Brien maintains, he would not have held out against O'Duffy over the issue of the New Irish Library. Yeats wanted a genuinely national theatre; he deplored propaganda but insisted that art could not be divorced from politics, and that Maud Gonne's marriage did not change his politics. Regarding Easter 1916, Cullingford suggests that Griffith's attacks on Yeats did not represent the Irish Republican Brotherhood, that Yeats helped to foster the romantic nationalist tradition, and that in the 1930s Yeats questioned the confusion of politics and theology – it was not 'wholesome for a people to think much of exceptional acts of faith or sacrifice' (Yeats, 1964, p. 266). In a chapter on 'Visionary Politics', Cullingford argues that *AV* is 'an exercise in symbolic politics', that Yeats was against both 'English materialist capitalism and Russian materialist socialism', and that he refused to move towards extremes either of determinism or of belief in free will. Yeats' interest in fascism is traced in a chapter entitled 'From Democracy to Authority'. By 1924 he was extremely interested in Italian fascism, and he began reading Croce and Gentile. While convalescing in Italy from February 1928 to summer 1930 he was favourably impressed by what he saw. Cullingford, in what is her least satisfactory chapter, apologises for Yeats and stresses his ignorance, or his superficial knowledge, or his misunderstanding of both Mussolini and Ireland. She suggests that Yeats' ideas were at variance with fascism, that Yeats' nationalism was in essence a 19th-century phenomenon, that Yeats was opposed to anti-semitism. Her chapter on the Senate is more sure and she identifies the major political problem for Yeats in these years (1922-8) as the reconciliation of the need for order with his desire for liberty. The Blue Shirts episode – the 'product of a temporary outburst of fanaticism' in Yeats – she relates to Yeats' 'fluctuating political estimate of De Valera'. The final years see a return to the old Fenian in Yeats, anti-English rather than pro-German, a nationalist of the school of O'Leary.

Cullingford argues forcefully against the view that Yeats was a fascist; she shows the interaction between day-to-day politics and Yeats' beliefs; she makes out a good case for seeing Morris as an important background presence in Yeats' politics; she insists that Yeats is a political writer; and she completely – or nearly completely – buries the last traces of O'Brien's argument. But certain doubts remain, not least O'Brien's concern that Yeats might have participated in a collaborationist regime in Dublin. Of course,this is unanswerable, but Cullingford's study does not in the end allay that nagging suspicion. What is missing from her book is a theoretical analysis of fascism and how this is related to 19th-century nationalism. She assumes in her first chapter, for example, that on the one side stands something wholesome called nationalism, and on the other there is the dreadful scourge we know as fascism. She wants to convince us that Yeats is a nationalist, and that his dalliance with fascism was superficial. But what needs to be investigated is the transition from 19th-century nationalism to 20th-century fascism. This is better handled in Craig (1981), and further discussed in ch. 6 of this study.

In a well-organised and often perceptive inquiry into Yeats and politics in the 1930s, Stanfield (1988) stresses the unity between poet, patriot and mystic, and insists on Yeats' politics and aesthetics being seen together. He traces the shifts in Yeats' attitude towards De Valera, particularly in the light of the poet's admiration for Parnell. De Valera was the inheritor of a political tradition in which Yeats had at first participated but which after 1903 he came to see as destructive; Catholic nationalism therefore needed Protestant leavening. Stanfield then charts Yeats' brief association with the Blue Shirts in the period from July 1933 to February 1934. Stanfield plays this down: his involvement was contemporary with other extravagant episodes in Yeats' life, such as the Steinach operation, the collaboration with Purohit or his sponsorship of Margot Ruddock. Among reasons for Yeats' disillusionment with fascism, Stanfield mentions the democratic bias of the Blue Shirts ('mob rule'), Yeats' fear that the Blue Shirts represented clerical autocracy, and his wider belief that fascism was but a finale to democracy and not a prelude to a new order. Fascism was relegated to the old 'primary' cycle. Stanfield devotes further chapters to Yeats, socialism and tragedy, Yeats and Balzac, and Yeats and eugenics. Throughout, he argues for the unity of Yeats' beliefs in the context both of the 1930s and of Yeats' life as a whole. Balzac appealed to Yeats because of his conservative propaganda and his occult interests. Balzac's emphasis on the family is linked with Yeats' belief in eugenics. According to Stanfield, Yeats' interest in eugenics was more than final vagary but represented long-held convictions about modern degeneration and the importance of birth and family. In his conclusion Stanfield maintains that the principles underlying Yeats' politics in the 1930s were already established prior to that decade. What was special about the 1930s was that Yeats' solitude increased and this in turn led to a desire to outrage. This is an intelligent contribution to the debate about Yeats and fascism, but it assumes a continuity in Yeats that has still to be proved. What are the origins of Yeats' political beliefs? What is the course of their development? Didn't the 1930s, didn't De Valera and the Blue Shirts, change Yeats' understanding of the principles underlying his politics? What part had Blake in the construction of Yeats' politics and is it significant that he is missing from this inquiry?

Other investigations by Farag (1978), McDiarmid (1984), Freyer (1981), Archibald (1983), Said (1988), Cronin (1982), Craig (1982) and Hassett (1986) have added to this discussion. Farag emphasises the indissoluble relation between Yeats' training in the Order of the Golden Dawn and his political stance. Yeats saw the double nature of things, and therefore had a double allegiance. Farag distinguishes Yeats' view of an elite from fascism, arguing – somewhat naively – that Yeats' interest in fascism was 'spiritual'. Yeats' final years were marked by disillusionment, a mixture of anarchism and bitter gaiety. In an unsophisticated comparative study of Yeats, Eliot and Auden between the Wars, McDiarmid stresses the common ground between the three writers, how civilisation could be saved via an identity based on inherited myths, legends and religious truths. Dismissing fascist labels as unhelpful, she charts a path from their enthusiasm and involvement in society to saving civilisation to rejection, and suggests that 'the wish for poetry to save the world dies hardest in Yeats'. What McDiarmid's study illustrates – leaving aside the cursory treatment of *AV* – is the difficulty of discussing Yeats' politics at one particular moment without reference to his development as a thinker and as a poet.

Freyer's more authoritative study outlines Yeats' involvement in politics and the critical reaction. Defending Yeats against the charge of fascism, Freyer sets his fascist views in the context of an anti-democratic tradition. Freyer stresses Yeats' Irishness, his determination to defend Ireland against England, his importance in creating in Ireland a consciousness of national identity, his defence of Ireland in the Casement ballads. Freyer points out that the parliamentary tradition in Ireland – although only established in 1922 – was strong enough to withstand fascism, that the Blue Shirts were not bidding for a fascist dictatorship, and that there is no trace of anti-semitism in Yeats' writings. These are all necessary observations, but there is a hesitancy about this book. Freyer promises to deal with the central issue but in effect does not, and it is still unclear at the end what constitutes the anti-democratic tradition, whether it is Irish or European, and how it relates to 19th-century nationalism. Archibald gives an intelligent account of Yeats' politics and the critical debate this question has provoked, and his comparison of Yeats and Burke is worth attention. Cronin takes issue with 'the narrow scholiasts' and insists – though he doesn't elaborate – that Yeats' vision of social order is 'no more like Hitler's or Mussolini's than it is like Melchizedek's', but is on the contrary more like Marx's. In a brief suggestive study Said describes Yeats as the national poet who represents the Irish nation in its war against tyranny. Yeats is a poet of decolonisation and associated therefore with Neruda, Cesaire and other modern poets involved in the resistance to imperialism. Yeats was a victim of nativism (an overvaluing of native Ireland in Yeats' case), a result of the colonial encounter with Britain, but he struggled to 'announce the contours of an "imagined" or ideal community', ever conscious of the instability of time. Moreover, Yeats made the first important announcement in the context of decolonisation of 'the need to balance violent force with an exigent political and organisational process'.

Hassett's study is an original and well-researched analysis into hatred in Yeats' work. Yeats belongs to a tradition of hatred as a source of creative activity which goes back to Swift and beyond. Hassett refers to Yeats' hatred of abstraction, to intellectual hatred and its deleterious effects on Ireland, and to Unity of Being as an answer. In a chapter on hatred as a Gnostic virtue, Hassett comments perceptively on Ribh's hatred and how Yeats knew this constituted only a beginning, that a responsible poetic intelligence was required once a new work or self was created. On the issue of violence and fascism in Yeats, Hassett examines three poems – 'Hound Voice', 'Leda and the Swan', and 'The Second Coming' – and defends them against the charge that Yeats welcomes universal bloodshed. Yeats cultivated hatred; but in writing a poem the poet ceases to hate, thus making a new self; love and hate are then restored to unmixed emotion, which in turn leads to radical innocence and the restoration of a fallen world.

Chapter 6

Yeats and the Contemporary Critical Perspective

Yeats and Literary Language

This particular topic has been addressed with varying results in three full-length studies by Beum (1969), Dougherty (1973) and Adams (1984) – though students should also refer to 'Yeats and the Literary Tradition' in ch. 5 above. Beum examines Yeats' metrics after 1910. In surveying the 236 poems collected between *WSC* and *LP*, Beum notices the following: the predominance of quatrains, sestets, octaves, song forms and free lyrics; the use of *ottava rima*, a form virtually untouched since Byron; the avoidance of all metres except iambic and trochaic; the absence of prosodic virtuoso pieces; relatively few examples of heroic couplet, little blank verse and no free verse; the extensive use of imperfect rhymes; how lines are end-paused; and how alliteration and assonance rarely become conscious. Beum describes Yeats as the great master of trochaic poetry. He also comments on slant rhyme as in 'The Gyres' and 'The Municipal Gallery Revisited', a poem whose third stanza contains not a single pure rhyme, indicative of Yeats' ear for variation in spoken English. Beum's best chapter – on Yeats' use of *ottava rima* – notices how, unlike the quatrain, the octave gave Yeats room, 'a larger stanza to carry the scope and penetration of a mature spirit'; it was both traditional and innovative; it also provided 'a reflective couplet for his increasing aphoristic bent and power; and like the Cowleian octave, it allowed resonant and incantatory effects'.

Dougherty analyses the rhythmic structure of Yeats' verse. Over half her book is devoted to statistical tables, which form the basis of her somewhat leaden discussion of metrical form and speech rhythms. Before 1903 Yeats preferred tetrameters, thereafter pentameters. As to stanzas, Yeats relied on end-rhymes, a feature of both his early and his later poetry; he borrowed the octave stanza from Cowley; he returned to the ballad form in *LP*. Dougherty concludes that Yeats is in the mainstream English tradition. Her discussion of speech rhythms, where she identifies Yeats' preference for rising cadences, is also fairly undistinguished. In her conclusion Dougherty emphasises that 'it is the verse-line that stands at the centre of Yeats' prosody as the controlling unit of the rhythmic structure'. She draws attention to the increase in system construction at the level of line and stanza in the later prosodic style and how this leads to a tension between the speech-unit and the verse line.

Adams, whose work is indebted to Gilles Deleuze and to post-structuralism in general and will be best appreciated in the light of contemporary linguistic theory, deliberately goes beyond the analysis of surface structure and concentrates on the way Yeats' syntax is also part of his Mask. He is concerned to identify the 'syntactic masks' in Yeats' verse, syntactic masks being a system composed of 'differential series', where two mutually exclusive syntactic alternatives occur simultaneously in the same words or phrase. Taking as his example the use of 'that' in restrictive and non-restrictive relative clauses, Adams suggests that Yeats' syntax runs counter to the poet's Platonism and actually presents us with 'difference' itself, for as a producer of subjectivity, the syntactic mask 'reverses the platonic view of the subject as producer of language'. In his first chapter on the noun phrase and determiner, Adams distinguishes between *situational* and *anaphoric* modes of determiners: in Yeats a determiner functioning situationally often embraces the anaphoric mode and vice-versa. In the clause 'I walk through the long schoolroom', the ostensible mode is situational, but this plays off against an anaphoric mode, since it is implied that the identity of the long schoolroom is already known to the narrator or reader. His chapter on noun phrase and modifier focuses on the play between the universal and the particular in phrases such as '*the* falcon cannot hear *the* falconer'. Citing Halliday, Adams also comments on Yeats' use of the *cataphoric* (or forward) reference of definite determiners. In 'the staggering girl' in 'Leda and the Swan', 'staggering' is not needed as identification, yet it tries to 'exercise its own defining power in the noun phrase', and thus becomes a mask, part of the play between defining and non-defining adjectives. Another chapter on relative clauses focuses on the fluctuation of the modifier between defining and non-defining roles, how there is often a play between the pause of a non-restrictive clause and the absence of pause associated with restrictive clauses. Adams' discussion of 'Labour is blossoming or dancing where/The body is not bruised to pleasure soul' is especially revealing and brings out the complex grammatical ambiguity that underlies Yeats' world-view at this point. A chapter on additive structuring explores Yeats' use of a syntactic chain that is not structured according to fixed grammatical relationships and where the elements hover between affiliation and separation: among his examples are 'News for the Delphic Oracle' and 'The Fisherman'. Adams also writes well about 'interrupters' in Yeats' verse, and how additive structuring by interruption can break up a text into 'segments that lose their univocal grammatical ties'. In a final chapter on Yeats' verb tenses, Adams notices the way masks of tense arise through use of an indefinite present tense in contexts where a definite form would be expected. In 'The unpurged images of day recede', the indefinite present tense runs counter to a definite moment of action and so becomes, in Adams' reading, a syntactic mask.

This is an illuminating study, although a little too brief to support the full implications of its theoretical argument. The idea of endless play, for example, needs further attention, for it is not absolutely certain that this leads to 'difference': it could be incorporated into a Platonic theory or into Yeats' belief that he needed to hammer his thoughts into unity. Equally, Adams needs a more inclusive or flexible framework, one that would be sensitive to the 'difference' as articulated in both Yeats and Joyce, for example, or one that addressed the relationship between metaphor and metonymy in Yeats' literary language. But this study highlights the ambiguity in Yeats' verse and shows that some difficulties belong not to Yeats' system of ideas, but to 'difference'.

Yeats and Women

Surprisingly, critics have largely ignored the issue of Yeats and women, content merely to repeat the conventional view that most references to women in Yeats' verse are to Maud Gonne. When feminist theory turns its attention to the complexities of Yeats, this should change. At present, there are too few studies, and we are still at the level of assessing the groundwork. For the subject of

Yeats and women covers not only the issue of biography, but also his characterisations of women, both in terms of imagery and mythology. There is, in addition, the more complex issue of feminine writing – writing not necessarily by women or about women but which works on the margins, stirs up differences, displaces authority. Criticism also needs to explore the distinction between 'women' as historical beings and 'woman' as a cultural construct and how this manifests itself in Yeats' work. In the meantime, both Webster (1974) and Kline (1983) are of interest, the one a crude Freudian account (see ch. 1 above), the other a Jungian interpretation, on which we can concentrate here.

Kline makes extensive use of Slochower's idea of the mythopoet (the poet who comes at the end of an era and recreates the idealism of its decaying social structures) and Neumann's concept of the great mother as archetype; Neumann's structural diagram of the archetypal feminine is her first illustration. She divides her study into four main areas: the myth, the personal quest, the cultural quest and a final recapitulation and critique. In her introduction Kline briefly traces Yeats' relationship with Maud Gonne, and suggests that Yeats never believed evil of her and that, once his infatuation was under control, she became for him a lasting poetic symbol.

In ch. 1 Kline investigates the concept of courtly love, its late 19th-century origins and its links with the woman lost. Before patriarchy there was matriarchy; the universe originated with the World Egg rather than the Word of the father. Women inspired men, who in turn conceived of them either positively, as the Muse or Divine Wisdom, or negatively as the Witch, Lilith or Circe. The early Yeats gravitates towards the feminine qualities in Western culture. Thus, woman is at first the Enchantress and later the Lady of Inspiration. In later life he took the masculine side, though in the figure of Crazy Jane we find the sympathetic appearance of the Great Mother. Kline comments on the presence of the mirror and the enclosed garden in Yeats' work, and notices how Yeats discards the mirror of Narcissus for the mirror of the Idea and how he moves between the gardens of the ruined and the restored Eden. In her chapter on the personal quest Kline ranges widely over Yeats' particular relationships with women. She comments on Yeats' mother, who represented the land of Ireland, 'earthy and mysterious' (but, even if this were true, Kline fails to notice how this might relate to her introversion); on Yeats' sexual awakening and the contrasts between *R* and *M*; on the way the women Yeats liked were women won, 'but the women he loved were women lost so that the imagination would remain stimulated'. She also discusses his relationship with Laura Armstrong, Olivia Shakespear, Katharine Tynan and Florence Farr, and compares the treatment of Laura in early works such as 'Time and the Witch Vivien' and *The Island of Statues* (the Virgin-enchantress) with that of Maud Gonne in *CK* (the Countess pursued by the troubadour Aleel/Kevin/Yeats). His male figures – witness 'The Cap and Bells', written in 1893 when his long separation from Maud began – gravitate towards self-destruction. George, however, brought Yeats' theories down to earth: in a poem such as 'A Prayer for My Daughter', a sermon preached to women, Kline descries Yeats the male poet who, for all his attention to the female image and to the feminine in himself, was always at heart masculine.

Kline then considers the cultural quest, again from the viewpoint of the courtly lover, and how the service of woman and the service of the Court became entwined in Yeats' mind. She comments on the influence of Lady Gregory, who read to him from Castiglione's *The Book of the Courtier* in the summer evenings of 1904 and who in April 1907 took him on a tour of Italian cities. According to Kline, Lady Gregory became a mother substitute for Yeats. She also examines the masculine and feminine elements in Yeats' Phases. Her diagram of the Great Year of Christianity makes clear the reversal of principles by which religious life, which begins in the feminine, becomes masculine, and secular life becomes feminine: in Phase 15 (c.1050) the Will and Creative Mind dominate religious life, precisely when the veneration of the Virgin Mary and courtly love begins. A final chapter looks at the last period of Yeats' life, the episode with Margot Ruddock and his relationship with Dorothy Wellesley, when a renewed urgency is placed on sexual activity, at the same time as images of madness occur. Kline compares the masculine and the feminine elements in the early and later Yeats, and she also explores the image of the Mother Goddess and the slain god in *The King of the Great Clock Tower* and *A Full Moon in March* and how these afforded a purgation for Yeats. Yeats ends his mythopoesis of courtly love by praising woman for using her mind: 'Yeats comprehended that a woman cannot have Unity of Being without her own intellect and that a man cannot have Unity of Being without recognising the feminine principle at work in himself'. Kline's is at once a useful and a problematic starting-point for analysing the subject of Yeats and women. The biographical information about the various women in Yeats' life is relevant and valuable, though far from comprehensive, and much more has still to come to light. The real difficulty stems from her interpretative approach. In terms of her own theory, for example, the large division she imposes between the personal and the cultural quest is not wholly suited to her purpose or her subject since it runs counter to Yeats' expressed intention to hammer his thoughts into unity. The use of myths and archetypes contains, I think, an inherent difficulty; namely how to make space for the actual course of Yeats' life and his particular relationships with individual women. Kline manages in part to resolve this dilemma by focusing on two distinct periods in Yeats' life – the 1880s and 1890s, and the 1930s – but many of her comments about Yeats' mother or the role of Lady Gregory as mother-substitute give the impression that she is dealing less with archetypes than with stereotypes.

Yeats and the Visual Arts

Henn's chapter 'Painter and Poet' (1950) is very helpful as an introduction to this particular topic. Henn touches on a number of relevant aspects: Yeats' use of pictorial symbolism, his debt to his father's ideas, the influence of his brother Jack, his predeliction for certain artists such as Blake and Calvert, and his antipathy to others such as Bastien-Lepage. The central section is devoted to identifying the visual sources for particular poems. The apparent arbitrariness in Yeats' use of visual sources 'can be seen as clearly related to his six great periods of human myth and history and thought: the "Babylonian starlight", the Greeks at the time of Phidias, Byzantium, the Quattrocento, the Renaissance, Blake'. Images beget fresh images, and thus it is that the Sphinx, for example, can be associated by Yeats with the Rock of Cashel. Yeats, Henn adds, was influenced more by the criticism of a painting than by the painting itself, and especially by Pater's *The Renaissance*. This three-part inquiry offers itself as a model: a survey of what is involved in such an inquiry, a detailed piece of detective work, and a more general discussion regarding the usefulness of such knowledge for an appreciation of the poetry. Later critics are indebted to Henn, even when like Clark (1983) they disagree with some of his findings.

Melchiori (1960) investigates the intellectual pattern upon which Yeats' poetry is built, and especially the linear or visual character of that pattern. He cautions against confusing visualness with natural beauty, for Yeats was not concerned with the description of landscapes, and in a separate observation he stresses the aesthetic side to Yeats' interest in the occult. Most of his chapters are devoted to tracking down visual sources, to noticing how they are used by Yeats and to commenting on their significance. In ch. 1 Melchiori discusses the beast and the unicorn and the apocalyptic sensibility that manifests itself in 'The Second Coming', *Where There is Nothing*, *The Player Queen*, and *AV*. Ch. 2 considers the image of Leda, the cyclical view of history and the links between the Trojan War, the birth of Christianity and some indefinite event in the present. He then traces the image of the swan in Yeats' work from Helen through Mary Hynes to the Tower. In the fourth chapter he returns to Leda and suggests that the myth was put into Yeats' mind in 1923 by Gogarty's 'An Offering of Swans' (Gogarty's thank-offering to the River Liffey for effectively saving him from his Republican captors). It was Moreau's *Licornes* that Yeats had in mind when writing 'Leda and the Swan' – not Michelangelo's *Leda and the Swan* as he mistakenly thought. Subsequent chapters on the mundane egg and the image of the dome (especially Byzantium) show an equally impressive mastery of the subject. In his final chapter Melchiori comments on the importance of Michelangelo, how the physical impact of the later poetry shows Yeats not as a myth-maker but as a creative artist, and how the whole mystery of art is essentially a movement from the visual to the intellectual plane. These various discussions are extremely valuable, but the underlying critical argument about the development of an idea into poetry is less sure.

Engelberg (1964), whose argument is that Yeats climbed out of the vast design of history towards the single image, makes two main points about Yeats and painting. Firstly, his work in drama enabled him to find a balance between gestures and the stasis associated with pictures; secondly, Yeats' interest in paintings enabled him to find some answers to his own aesthetic problems. Thus Blake and Whistler provided a convenient pair of antithetical artists and helped him clarify his reponses to symbolism, *symbolisme* and imagism. Yeats learnt through images and gestures to find dramatic intensity, especially evident in 'Byzantium'. The final reconciliation between the motion and rest of reality can be seen in 'The Statues', which celebrates the single image of art as it climbs out of the vast design of history. Engelberg's thesis is relatively straightforward, but occasionally it is hard to distinguish the wood from the trees. His work underlines the need for a coherent view of Yeats' aesthetic theory and suggests how dramatic gesture and visual stasis can be related.

Loizeaux's highly commendable survey (1986) of Yeats and the visual arts concentrates on the development of Yeats' verse in the light of his changing understanding of art. She stresses the Pre-Raphaelite influence on the early Yeats, then the movement towards sculpture away from the pictorial qualities of art. In essence her book traces the path from poem-as-picture to poem-as-sculpture. Her first chapter on Yeats and the Pre-Raphaelites outlines the importance of the artistic movement and how it defined the task for his own poetry in the context of painting. In her second chapter on Yeats' early poetic theory, Loizeaux observes that pictures afforded a corrective to abstraction but that Yeats also associated poetry with vision. This leads into a discussion of symbolism and how a poem's ecstatic emotion is symbolised in a definite imagined region, far from the cares of the world. The following chapter explores these early poetic regions as expressed in *The Island of Statues*, *WO*, and *WR*. Here Loizeaux detects in *WO* the influence of Morris, especially in the symbolic potential of landscape, and how *WR* represents a turning towards Ireland for his landscape. She makes a useful distinction when discussing the relationship between symbol and reality: 'in Yeats' finest poems the symbolic landscape never takes precedence over the landscape as experienced'.

Ch. 4 traces the passage of Yeats' idea of drama from picture to sculpture, how Craig inspired the former, and Pound and Dulac the latter. Loizeaux interestingly observes that a single problem motivated all Yeats' experiments in set design: how to stage the world of imagination, to picture the soul. But his early poetic pictures lacked dramatic force for stage presentation. Here was the paradox, for Yeats wanted both remoteness and nearness. It was Nugent Monck's 1911 production of *CK* which showed Yeats how sculpture could be used as a dramatic model. Pound with his enthusiasm for Epstein and Gaudier-Brzeska, combined with the work of Dulac as designer for the Noh plays, edged Yeats closer to sculpture. The consequences are explored in the following chapter, where Loizeaux claims that Yeats became a more profound Pre-Raphaelite, desiring a unity not just with the arts but with culture as a whole. The changes between 1911 and 1925 become particularly apparent both in *AV* and in his later poetry. *AV* contains a history of art, where Yeats positions himself in a phase that stresses sculpture. His later poetry is written out of a clear understanding of his aesthetic aims and with a firm grasp of his craft; the visual arts now enter the poetry explicitly and consistently. Loizeaux's sixth chapter on the visual arts in the later poetry considers the most important aesthetic issue of these later poems, namely the function of art as monument, the permanence of art versus the impermanence of man. 'Yeats' late poetry replaces the passive dream reflections of Buddha, Byzantium, and the Pre-Raphaelites with an art of the body that actively affects its audience.' A final chapter on the idea of sculptural poetry explores the use of space, the way the subject-object dichotomy diminishes, the depiction of the human body as a normal subject, the image of the self after life, and the sculptural effect of the late verse and how it creates a sense of spatial and temporal immediacy. This is a very valuable book. Replete with carefully chosen illustrations, it offers a reading of Yeats' verse in the light of his changing understanding of painting and sculpture.

Yeats and Modern Literature

Yeats and Nietzsche

The links between Yeats and Nietzsche have been extensively explored in recent criticism. It is a topic that actually subsumes other areas often dealt with separately, as for example Literary Parnellism (see Howarth, 1958 or Brown, 1972), the figure of Cuchulain, concepts such as the heroic ideals (see Zwerdling, 1965), or tragic joy. Ellmann (1954) touches on most of the points investigated in more detail by subsequent inquiries: the relevance of Nietzsche for the development of Yeats' cyclical theory; the place of Blake vis-à-vis Yeats and Nietzsche; the issue of debt or parallel in concepts such as the Doctrine of the Mask or the

Nietzschean superman; Yeats' rejection (or otherwise) of Nietzsche's extremism; the edition of Nietzsche that Yeats used. Yeats was presented with a copy of Thomas Common's 1901 edition of Nietzsche by his American patron John Quinn, in which he made copious marginal notes. These have continued to interest Yeats scholars. Thatcher (1970), in a survey of Nietzsche's reputation in England in 1890-1914, considers the references to Nietzsche in Yeats' work, the annotations in the Common edition, and the parallels between the two writers. According to Thatcher, Yeats – already under the influence of Blake and Shelley – was immune to Nietzsche's more extreme views, though he was fascinated by the distinction between slave- and master-morality and by the figure of the superman. Thatcher argues forcefully against Ellmann (1954) and Wilson (1960) and claims that nowhere 'does Yeats explicitly repudiate the superman idea'. Thatcher also explores the Nietzschean idea of self-overcoming, a concept that Yeats 'was to make his own'. Self-conquest entails the joyful acceptance of a formidable challenge and the obligation on the part of the individual to overcome moral and spiritual failings. Such an idea is particularly apparent in the double movement of the gyres, one towards self-abnegation, the other towards self-affirmation, the tension in other words between the saint and the superhuman. Self-conquest can also be seen in the Doctrine of the Mask, in Yeats' political hopes for a new caste of leaders, and in the obligation to destroy all hollow religious idols and thereby 'transvalue all values'.

Bridgwater (1972) examines the influence, debts and parallels that exist between Nietzsche and various modern writers including Yeats. In his discussion of the Common edition, Bridgwater covers similar ground to Thatcher. As to the Nietzschean echoes in Yeats' verse and drama, Bridgwater suggests this is most clearly seen in the plays written between 1903 and 1910, especially *Where There is Nothing* and *The Hour Glass*. Nietzsche had less impact on his verse, but can be observed in lines such as 'Homer is my example and his unchristened heart', in poems such as 'Lapis Lazuli', 'The Second Coming', and in ideas about aristocratic morality. According to Bridgwater, Yeats went through two Nietzschean phases – 1903-21 and 1930-9. Nietzsche is a less important influence than, say, Plotinus, and Yeats ultimately condemned

Nietzsche for his pessimism, but only after spending much of his intellectual life in his company.

O'Brien (1972) in a series of lectures on Machiavelli, Burke, Nietzsche and Yeats, four writers linked by 'the suspecting glance', takes issue with the gentle Nietzscheans, who seek to underline the spiritual side to Nietzsche's work (e.g. his scorn of Germany, his contempt for anti-semites). For O'Brien, any spiritual revolution advocated by the gentle Nietzschean requires a political revolution – and Nietzsche claimed that perfection in politics is Machiavellianism. It is not surprising, according to O'Brien, that Nietzsche was so highly regarded by the Nazis, for Nietzsche is 'the most radically anti-semitic writer...known to history', who 'made it easier for Nazism to pursue its inner logic as far as the gas chambers'. In a final lecture on Burke, Nietzsche and Yeats, O'Brien adverts to Yeats' father's belief that the whole of Nietzsche was malign, and goes on to argue against Ellmann's view that Yeats discarded the brutal implications of Nietzsche's ethics, claiming that it was impossible for Yeats to 'remain altogether unaffected by the fierceness, which is so central to Nietzsche's writings'. Yeats' reading of Nietzsche, which coincided with Maud Gonne's marriage in 1903, prepared the way for his rift with the nationalist movement, and signalled his break with the liberal attitude of mind of Lady Gregory, his father and most of his friends. With particular reference to 'Upon a House Shaken by the Land Agitation' (1910), 'The Phases of the Moon' (1917) and 'Blood and the Moon' (1928), O'Brien outlines the path from gentle to fierce Nietzscheanism. O'Brien makes explicit what he sees as the links between Nietzsche and Nazism on the one hand, and between Nietzsche and Yeats' increasingly right-wing politics on the other. In its own way his inquiry is a continuation of his earlier study (1965) (see ch. 5 above), and it is not without influence as can be seen for example in Davie's essay on the fascism of 'Blood and the Moon' (Davie, 1980). The problem with O'Brien's analysis is that it is too narrowly conceived, and fails to do justice to the 'human' Yeats that Ellmann, Donoghue (1968) and others rightly insist upon; it also ties up too neatly the passage of ideas from the 19th century to their enactment in the 20th century, and lacks the theoretical sophistication to tackle the relationship between aesthetics and politics.

Bohlmann (1982) provides a very readable, full-length account of Yeats and Nietzsche, which if it errs does so on the side of scepticism. It is impossible, Bohlmann writes, 'to determine beyond all doubt the point at which similarities cease to be coincidental and become testimony to direct influence'; Yeats was 'an incipient Nietzschean long before he encountered Nietzsche'. But, if extended, this view would obviously question the initial attempt to yoke them together. Bohlmann argues that Nietzsche played a role in toughening Yeats' outlook in 1903-14; he follows O'Brien in distinguishing between harsh and gentle Nietzscheans; and his comments are often suggestive, as when he claims that the concept of eternal recurrence is more benign than Yeats' gyres.

Yeats and modernism

Contemporary critics are frequently unsure of Yeats' place in the context of modernism. Indeed, recent inquiries into the aesthetics of modernism by Levenson (1984), Schwartz (1986) and Chefdor (1986) almost completely ignore the work of Yeats. In the 1930s Leavis (1932) pioneered the view that Yeats belongs with Eliot and Pound in the development of the modern movement in verse (see the section on Yeats' lineage in ch. 2 above). The word 'modernist' was not in Leavis' vocabulary, and it is only recently that it has been applied to Yeats: in the 1960s Yeats was a modern – as opposed to a contemporary – poet. If Brooks were re-writing his *Modern Poetry and the Tradition* (1939) he would perhaps be tempted to call it 'Modernist Poetry and the Tradition'. Writing in 1960 Rosenthal had no difficulty in affirming that Yeats was the least experimental of the great modern poets; today, he would be forced into closer definition or defence of his terms or position. The shift from modern to modernist, briefly alluded to in Bergonzi (1986) – a study which also ignores Yeats – has given a closer definition to a literary movement but it is not without its attendant difficulties. Certain questions become more troubling: when did modernism begin and end? Which writers belong to it? Is it a badge worn by individuals or does it cover the whole age? Modernism, according to Spears (1970), is 'an impossible subject'. Not surprisingly, in the light of what has been said elsewhere in this book, Yeats – always at once out of place and yet central – resists the narrow definitions of critical orthodoxy, whether past or present (see Lentricchia,

1968). Nevertheless, the attempt to enlist him into the modernist camp often sheds new light on both modernism and Yeats.

Certain lines of interpretation, such as what might be termed the Romanticisation of Modernism – the attempt to ground modernism in the earlier literary movement – have never been far from the surface of modern criticism. Thus, Brooks (1939) claimed that Yeats and Eliot built on the Romantic tradition; Hough (1947), following the poet's own description of himself, called Yeats one of the last Romantics; Kermode (1957) sees modern poetry as the latest in line from Romanticism. 'Make it new' was Pound's advice to aspiring poets, but one line of critics have refused to believe modernism was that new. In a sense it is easier to see Yeats as belonging to modernism if its roots in Romanticism are emphasised, but if modernism is defined by its use of revolutionary avant-garde techniques then Yeats does not quite belong. It is for this reason that Leavis, who insists on modern poetry's complete break with Victorianism, has difficulty siting Yeats, especially the early Yeats. This becomes even more apparent in a critic such as Stead, whose Leavisite inheritance – at once so enabling and disabling – has recently emerged with a vengeance.

In his first study (1964) Stead emphasises the newness of Yeats and Eliot, how Yeats faced and resolved the problem of distance between poet and audience, at the same time integrating his diverse subject-matter, and how Eliot, especially in his theory, tackled the Romantic inheritance. In order to overthrow the discursiveness of Victorian verse, both poets gravitated towards the Image, conscious of the need to avoid the isolation of aesthetic and moral qualities in poetry. They embarked on the reconciliation of two impulses, Image and discourse; an enterprise, Stead suggests, that constitutes the new poetic. In his more recent study (1986), Stead seeks to drive a wedge between Eliot and Pound who were modernists, and Yeats and Hardy who were moderns but not modernists. Stead's new complaint against Yeats is that, in contrast with Pound's experimentalism, he is enslaved to fixed forms, unable to write free verse and anything longer than the short lyric. In a series of detailed comparisons between individual poems, including 'Prufrock' and 'These are the Clouds', on the one hand, and 'Mauberley', 'Gerontion' and 'In Memory of Major Robert Gregory', on the other, Stead is intent on demonstrating the weakness of Yeats' verse and the strength of the modernists.

In a chapter comparing Yeats and Hardy, Stead highlights the contrasts between the mythologised Maud Gonne and the domestic Emma; he notices how the two poets deal differently with ideas in their verse, criticises 'Meditations in Time of Civil War' for its want of thought, and concludes that Yeats is a superior poet to Hardy; this last remark accompanies the Poundian rebuff he cites earlier that Yeats was 'the greatest minor poet who ever lived'. Unfortunately, all these discriminations tend to rebound on Stead and merely serve to expose the narrow base of his own critical position, preoccupied as it is with rank-ordering and with shrinking the orbit of modernism. That Yeats does not fit into modernism – whether Stead's restricted view of it or some other – is for me one of the poet's strengths, for he thereby challenges us to make sense of his work in terms other than those of discourse and Image, or free verse and experimentalism, forcing us to pay equal attention to his discontinuity both with his contemporaries and with the past.

Stead's analysis of 'Pound v. Yeats' should be read alongside Longenbach's stimulating, 'corrective' study of Yeats and Pound during the three winters between 1913 and 1916 they spent together at Stone Cottage. 'Although Pound is often thought of as a poet who dragged the reluctant Yeats into the twentieth century, the actual turns of influence reveal Yeats as the dominant force.' Longenbach brings out how Yeats belonged to the same movement as Pound. Pound's private conception of Imagism in terms of the 'Doctrine of the Image', as outlined in 'Ikon', a prose poem of December 1913, is Yeatsian in both language and sentiment. Yeats helped Pound clarify the esoteric aspect of symbols, how 'the image is the word beyond formulated language'. Longenbach also draws attention to the occult origins of *The Cantos* and to the 'secret society' of modernism to which both writers subscribed. He shows how the connection between Irish folklore, the Noh and the occult provided a turning-point in both their careers: '*Four Plays for Dancers*, *Per Amica Silentia Lunae*, and the early *Cantos* each in its own way grew from their collaborative research at Stone cottage'. Pound admired Yeats for his stand against the public, for the 'nobility' of his verse. Longenbach includes a discussion of their responses to the First World War, and how both desired to forge a new order for the post-war world. 'The Grey Rock', in its juxtaposition of mythic and modern narratives and in its conception of the 1890s tragic generation, anticipates a later modernist poem such as *Hugh Selwyn Mauberley*; more generally, Yeats played an important part in establishing a genealogy of modernism for Pound and Eliot. The influence was not all one way: Yeats needed Pound's admiration during a period of insecurity in his poetic career; equally, he associated Pound with his anti-self. In his concluding remarks, Longenbach makes a useful distinction: while Yeats was rarely an exemplar of modernist sensibility, 'he was a constant model for the noble mission of an artistic elite and a direct connection to its aristocratic heritage'. Finally, he wonders if the excesses of *On the Boiler* and Pound's radio broadcasts are not 'the inevitable conclusion of the anti-democratic attitudes fostered in such secluded places as Stone Cottage'.

In a closely argued account of Yeats, Eliot and Pound, Craig (1981) takes a different tack and outlines modernism's debt not to the Romantic movement but to late 18th-century associationist ideas, and how this is especially apparent in the priority assigned to memory over imagination. 'Associationist theory is not an account of how art comes into existence, but of how our experience of art is different from our experience of anything not art.' Yeats, according to Craig, belongs not to the school of romantic symbolists but rather to the associationist theory of aesthetics, especially as formulated in the work of Archibald Alison. 'In Memory of Major Robert Gregory' he interprets not as a romantic aesthetic of apocalypse but as concerned with the art of memory: it is not Gregory's fight with his times that is upheld in the poem, but rather the realisation that memory will have to supplant imagination. 'The man of memory (Yeats), living by the values of time, opposes the man of imagination (Gregory), who will be shown trapped in the values of space.' In a later chapter Craig distinguishes between the romantic and the associationist view of alienation; the former stemmed from the loss of contact with the universe, but with the latter it is loss of memory which is the dominant fear. Yeats is haunted after 1900 by the erosion and loss of memory, which he only gradually recovers in the years after 1912 by reference to the Great Memory and the public events of his time, especially the Easter Rising. Yeats' turning towards fascism in the 1920s is therefore interpreted by Craig within the context of the destruction of the Anglo-Irish and the consequent loss of those images which unite the nation.

This is an unconventional but suggestive reading of Yeats and modernism, which is worth dwelling on. In my view Yeats was more influenced by O'Grady's 'great enchantment' thesis than by any theory about loss of memory. In a series of articles in *All Ireland Review* beginning in January 1900, O'Grady suggested that 'the political understanding of Ireland today is under a spell, and its will paralysed...the hour when Ireland must either break the spell or sink for ever into the abyss prepared for all the nations who have forgotten the source of their life...is drawing nigh'. This seems to me the context for the opening of 'Easter 1916', with Ireland under a spell, in 'an enchanted condition'. The lines 'All changed, changed utterly:/A terrible beauty is born' do not imply, as Craig claims, 'the speaker's despair in the face of what has occurred'. In fact 'Easter 1916', with its duplication of words and images, is a not so subtle reworking of O'Grady's 'great enchantment'. Thus, O'Grady begins with references to enchantment in history, then enchantment in nature (how in a stone a man will see a flashing diamond and in a flashing diamond a stone), how Ireland in 1853 – 'the great betrayal' O'Grady calls it – was under a spell, unable to stop Westminster imposing financial burdens on the country. Yeats begins with history – the 18th century – turns to nature in the third stanza (and, as in O'Grady, he twice refers to 'stone'), and elaborates on the theme of 'betrayal' in the Anglo-Irish context. Of course, Yeats does more with the idea: for O'Grady 'enchantment' is 'obsession', while for Yeats it exists within a more complex debate about commitment and transformation (whether seen in terms of historical and political change, or of writing and the imagination), but the great enchantment thesis has much to recommend it. Enchantment could be read as an example of loss of memory, but I think it more properly qualifies such a concept and resurrects a different line of discussion that takes its bearings from Carlyle and O'Grady and that centres not on the linear sequence of history or how that might be recovered but on history's radical breaks and ruptures.

Yeats and modern culture

Contemporary critical accounts of Yeats – such as those by Sisson (1981) or Lucas (1986) in their surveys of modern English poetry – often say very little that is new. In his study of Yeats, Eliot and R.S. Thomas, Dyson (1981) concentrates on a close reading of poems from the major phase 1916-39. With the help of Jeffares' *Commentary*, Dyson examines in turn the success of 'An Irish Airman foresees his Death' in terms of its neutral tone between despair and exhilaration; the possibility of understanding a poem like 'Ego Dominus Tuus' without recourse to the philosophy of *AV*; Yeats' multivalent attitude to England in 'Easter 1916'; the clumsiness in the transition from the eighth to the ninth stanza in 'A Prayer for my Daughter'. Throughout, he stresses not the biographical or compositional elements but the finished poem, its opening tones and ambivalence; some poems he considers in terms of their chronology rather than their order in a particular collection; he frequently cites Jung and the Geneva School, and he includes reactions of his students. But his approach is somewhat leaden, and while the attention to detail and insistence on complexity are commendable, a close reading of Yeats can only take us so far. Yeats' career as a poet demands a higher level of abstraction, of interpretation, than that afforded by the critical orthodoxy we might associate with I.A. Richards.

Contemporary critics are still exercised by the question of Yeats' relationship with other writers. Yeats himself, as can be seen in his careful placing of writers in *AV*, or in his personal choices for the *Oxford Book of Modern Verse* (1936) showed them the way. Students might begin with Ellmann's inquiry (1970) into Yeats' links with Wilde, Joyce, Pound, Eliot and Auden, for Ellmann's unravelling of the biographical strands reminds us of Yeats' centrality in any discussion of modern writers. Those interested in pursuing the subject of Yeats and the political poets of the 1930s – beyond the outline given in ch. 2 above – might consult Hynes (1972), who writes well about 'Lapis Lazuli' as a 'parable of the politics beyond politics'. Yeats, whose tragic vision became more relevant as the decade unfolded, offered the younger poets of the Thirties 'an example of a profound poetic response' to calamities beyond individual human powers. Diggory's survey of Yeats and American poetry (1983) explores the 19th-century tradition of the self in Whitman and how this was reconstituted in the 20th century as the four-fold division of natural speech, created being, the communal self and private experience. In the 1910s, Pound's stress on the central importance of speech for poetry had an impact not only on Yeats but also on American poets; in the 1920s, in the work of Eliot especially, the self is felt to be artificial and in need of being remade by tradition. In the 1930s, poets (especially Southern Agrarians such as Tate and Ransom) saw similarities between the South and Ireland; to them Yeats was locked in a similar battle against the disintegration of the old order, ever conscious of the need for public speech. In the 1940s, the tradition of the self reached its climax in confessional poetry, but, in contrast to Yeats, American poets such as Berryman and Lowell became conscious that coherence no longer resided in the self. Diggory ends by stressing what American poets can learn from Yeats – that revelation is not merely of the self but is from the self.

We can conclude with two studies that underline Yeats' centrality in any discussion about modern culture and the continuing crisis of the unitary subject. Hillis Miller (1966), in an analysis of modern culture as revealed in the work of Conrad, Yeats, Eliot, Dylan Thomas, Stevens and Carlos Williams, questions the assumption that 20th-century poetry is merely an extension of Romanticism. 19th-century writers accepted the dichotomy between subject and object; they were no longer able to experience God as immanent and transcendent; God was there but He had disappeared. In the 20th century 'God is dead'; technology is triumphant and humanity even forgets it has murdered God. Moving against this direction of history has been the nihilism in modern literature. What links Miller's chosen writers is their acceptance of nihilism, by which means they enter a new reality – Yeats by affirmation of the infinite richness of the finite moment, Eliot by the discovery that Incarnation is here and now, Thomas by the acceptance of death, Stevens by the identification of imagination and reality in the poetry of being, Williams by his plunge into the 'filthy Passaic'. Yeats begins with an attempt to unite the human soul and the soul of the world, but, driven by his vision of eternal beauty, he finds the self is condemned to chase itself eternally, and he comes to realise that the saint and the artist are incompatible. In *AV* the contraries in Yeats' nature are expressed in terms of reality and justice, reality being defined by Miller as the irrational intensity of actual experience and justice as the hidden law behind it. Yeats is obsessed with the tragedy of human involvement in time, and hence his concern with apocalypse, with the concept of the eternal return, with the prospect of reincarnation, with escaping the terror of history by affirming that everything is inevitable. Time can be redeemed by being reversed, re-enacted, or by the process of Dreaming Back. But freedom can be attained only by denying any hope of reaching heaven, and by accepting tragic joy and the fact that every moment of life can be a divine centre. Because 'man can embody the truth' he can thereby free himself from the horror of eternal return. In conclusion, Miller adds, Yeats has provided an unexpectedly successful recovery of immanence; the supernatural is revealed in every corner of life. Far from being a Platonist, Yeats celebrates the way down, how liberation comes from battle, drunkenness, rage, sex and art. This is an original interpretation of Yeats. It is difficult to do justice to it in summary, but it offers insights which have still to be absorbed in Yeats criticism.

Langbaum (1977), whose study underpins Diggory's, considers the theme of identity in modern literature. Taking six different modern writers, Langbaum traces the passage from loss to reconstitution of the self. The first four writers illustrate the loss of self: Wordsworth reveals the self as process; Arnold is the first Victorian poet to deal with the modern problem of the loss of the self; in T.S. Eliot, 'the self is buried even deeper than in Arnold and is even less individual'; Beckett, whose work is like a report on humanity, pursues the inaccessible self. The self is reconstituted in the work of Lawrence and Yeats. Yeats was obsessed with finding an identity not through self-realisation but through the Anti-Self. He was involved therefore in a perpetual struggle to transform the self into a work of art. For Yeats, revelation is from the self; the greatest artists fulfil themselves in life and art by using art to mythologise their lives; self-realisation may require a succession of historical periods and a succession of lives; in *AV* Yeats draws an analogy between personality and art, and he reads history as primarily art history. Langbaum then focuses on the self as God, on the images of transformation in Yeats' verse. He notices, for example, the movement from living to mythological figures in poems such as 'Easter 1916' or 'A Dialogue of Self and Soul' and how this is reversed in 'The Municipal Gallery Revisited' or 'A Bronze Head'. *LP* is 'mainly about the transformation of perspective and identity resulting from assimilation to the Great Mind and Great Memory'; *The Death of Cuchulain* answers most completely the issue of identity Yeats had wrestled with ever since *The Player Queen*, namely the passage from flesh-and-blood creature to mythical person. Although less arresting than Miller's, this study underlines Yeats' significance as a cultural thinker and resites the discussion of the Primary and Antithetical Self within the wider context of modern identity.

No survey of Yeats criticism, as is evident from scanning the two leading annual journals devoted exclusively to Yeats – one edited in London by Warwick Gould, the other in New Orleans by Richard Finneran – would be complete without some reference to the international community of scholars that the poet has brought together. As a glance at the bibliography confirms – see also Jochum's bibliography (1978) – Yeats is the subject of attention throughout the world, from Japan and India across Europe to America. Unlike Joyce, for example, he is not at the vortex of the new theory that takes its cue from deconstruction, post-structuralism or feminism, but, as is especially evident from the section on 'Autobiography' in ch. 4 above, his work does lend itself to such readings. Equally, if this book is dominated by American scholarship, and if my own reading of Yeats emphasises the poet's Irishness, it is worth remembering here the European dimension. In Ireland the International Yeats Summer School for students is held every summer in Sligo; annual conferences of the International Association of Irish Studies – and the conferences of their respective member countries – often include papers on Yeats; in Halle in the German Democratic Republic the biannual international conference on Irish culture, organised by Dorothea Siegmund-Schultze (1987), normally sees papers on Yeats; the Federal Republic of Germany, as is attested to by Jochum's magnificent bibliography of Yeats criticism, also has a strong interest in the poet; in France Patrick Rafroidi and Yves Bonnefoy have been writing on Yeats and Irish literature since the early 1960s; in Italy Giorgio Melchiori has been for many years an important focus for Yeats and Joyce studies while the work of a younger generation of scholars, such as Anthony Johnson at Pisa, is also becoming influential; in Britain the publishing activity of Colin Smythe has put all Yeatsians in his debt. Gradually, a European perspective on Yeats is taking shape, which in time will make itself felt, and perhaps come to challenge – albeit in a friendly way – the current pre-eminence of American scholarship in this area.

Bibliography

Cross references are marked *

Abrams, M.H., *Natural Supernaturalism: Tradition and Revolution in Romantic Literature* (1971; Norton, 1973)
Adams, H., *Blake and Yeats: The Contrary Vision* (1955; reissued Russell and Russell, 1968)
Adams, J., *Yeats and the Masks of Syntax* (Macmillan, 1984)
Albright, D., *The Myth Against Myth: A Study of Yeats' Imagination in Old Age* (Oxford University Press, 1972)
Allen, J.L., *Yeats' Epitaph: A Key to Symbolic Unity in his Life and Work* (University Press of America, 1982)
Archibald, D., *Yeats* (Syracuse University Press, 1983)
Arnold, M., *On the Study of Celtic Literature* (Smith, Elder and Co., 1867)
Auden, W.H., 'The Public v. the Late Mr W.B. Yeats' (1939), repr. *Pritchard (1972), pp. 136-42
—— 'In Memory of W.B. Yeats' (1939a), repr. *Pritchard (1972), pp. 143-5
Bentley, E., *In Search of Theater* (Dennis Dobson, 1954)
Bergonzi, B., *The Myth of Modernism and Twentieth Century Literature* (Harvester Press, 1986)
Beum, R., *The Poetic Art of W.B. Yeats* (Ungar, 1969)
Bjersby, B., *The Interpretation of the Cuchulain Legend in the Works of W.B. Yeats* (Almqvist and Wiksells Boktryckeri, 1950)
Blackmur, R.P., 'The Later Poetry of W.B. Yeats' (1936), repr. in *Language as Gesture: Essays in Poetry* (George Allen and Unwin, 1954)
Bloom, H., *Yeats* (Oxford University Press, 1970)
Bohlmann, O., *Yeats and Nietzsche: An Exploration of Major Nietzschean Echoes in the Writings of William Butler Yeats* (Barnes and Noble, 1982)
Bornstein, G., *Yeats and Shelley* (Chicago University Press, 1970)
—— *Transformations of Romanticism in Yeats, Eliot, and Stevens* (University of Chicago Press, 1976)
Bowra, C.M., *The Heritage of Symbolism* (1943; repr. UK: Macmillan; USA: St Martin's Press, 1959)

Boyd, E., *Ireland's Literary Renaissance* (Alfred Knopf, 1922)
Bradford, C., *Yeats at Work* (Southern Illinois University Press, 1965)
— (ed.), *W.B. Yeats: The Writing of* The Player Queen (Northern Illinois University Press, 1971)
Bridgwater, P., *Nietzsche in Anglosaxony: A Study of Nietzsche's Impact on English and American Literature* (Leicester University Press, 1972)
Brooks, C., *Modern Poetry and the Tradition* (1939; repr. Oxford University Press, 1965)
— and Warren, R.P., *Understanding Poetry* (Holt, 1938)
Brown, M., *The Politics of Irish Literature: From Thomas Davis to W.B. Yeats* (George Allen and Unwin, 1972)
Bushrui, S.B., *Yeats' Verse Plays: The Revisions, 1900-1910* (Claredon Press, 1965)
Chefdor, M. et al (eds), *Modernism: Challenges and Perspectives* (University of Illinois Press, 1986)
Clark, D., *W.B. Yeats and the Theatre of Desolate Reality* (Dolmen Press, 1965)
— *Yeats at Songs and Choruses* (Colin Smythe, 1983)
Common, T., *Nietzsche as Critic, Philosopher, Poet and Prophet* (Grant Richards, 1901)
Cosgrave, P., 'Yeats, Fascism and Conor O'Brien', *London Magazine*, July 1967, pp. 22-41
Craig, C., *Yeats, Eliot, Pound and the Politics of Poetry* (Croom Helm, 1981)
Croker, T.C., *Researches in the South of Ireland* (1824; repr. Irish University Press, 1968: introd. K. Danagher)
— *Fairy Legends and Traditions of the South of Ireland* (John Murray, 1834; 1st ed. 1825-8)
Cronin, A., *Heritage Now: Irish Literature in the English Language* (Brandon, 1982)
Cross, K.G.W. and Dunlop, R.T., *A Bibliography of Yeats Criticism 1887-1965* (Macmillan, 1971)
Crowley, A., *Moonchild: A Prologue* (Mandrake Press, 1929)
Cullingford, E., *Yeats, Ireland and Fascism* (Macmillan,1981)
— (ed.), *Yeats: Poems, 1919-1935* (Macmillan, 1984)
Curtin, J., *Myths and Folklore of Ireland* (Sampson Low, 1890)
Daiches, D., *Poetry in the Modern World: A Study of Poetry in England Between 1900 and 1939* (Chicago University Press, 1940; Yeats chapter repr. in *Hall and Steinmann, 1950, pp. 106-24)
— 'The Practical Visionary', *Encounter* 108, Sept. 1962, pp. 71-4
Davie, D., *Trying to Explain* (Carcanet New Press, 1980)

Deane, S., *Celtic Revivals: Essays in Modern Irish Literature 1880-1980* (Faber, 1987)
de Man, P., *Allegories of Reading: Figural Language in Rousseau, Nietzsche, Rilke and Proust* (Yale University Press, 1979)
— *The Rhetoric of Romanticism* (Columbia University Press, 1984)
Diggory, T., *Yeats and American Poetry: The Tradition of the Self* (Princeton University Press, 1983)
Domville, E. (ed.), *A Concordance to the Plays of W.B. Yeats*, 2 vols (Cornell University Press, 1972)
Donoghue, D., *The Third Voice: Modern British and American Verse Drama* (USA: Princeton University Press; UK: Oxford University Press, 1959)
— and Mulryne, J.R. (eds), *An Honoured Guest: New Essays on W.B. Yeats* (Edward Arnold, 1965)
— *The Ordinary Universe: Soundings in Modern Literature* (Faber, 1968)
— *Yeats* (Fontana, 1971)
— 'Being Irish Together', *The Sewanee Review*, vol. lxxxiv no. 1, Jan.-March 1976, pp. 129-33
—'Textual Choices', *The Times Higher Educational Supplement*, 8 June 1984, p. 20
Dorn, K., *Players and Painted Stage: The Theatre of W.B. Yeats* (UK: Harvester Press; USA: Barnes and Noble, 1984)
— 'Dialogue into Movement: W.B. Yeats' Theatre Collaboration with Gordon Craig', in *O'Driscoll and Reynolds (1975), pp. 109-38
Dougherty, A., *A Study of Rhythmic Structure in the Verse of William Butler Yeats* (Mouton, 1973)
Dyson, A.E., *Yeats, Eliot, and R.S. Thomas: Riding the Echo* (Macmillan, 1981)
Eisenstadt, S.N., *Tradition, Change and Modernity* (John Wiley, 1973)
Eliot, T.S., 'Yeats' (1940), repr. in *On Poetry and Poets* (Faber, 1957)
Ellis-Fermor, U., *The Irish Dramatic Movement* (Methuen, 1939)
Ellmann, R., *Yeats the Man and the Masks* (1948; repr. Faber, 1973)
— *The Identity of Yeats* (1954; repr. Faber, 1964)
— *Eminent Domain: Yeats Among Wilde, Joyce, Pound, Eliot and Auden* (Oxford University Press, 1970)
— *Four Dubliners: Wilde, Yeats, Joyce and Beckett* (1987; repr. Sphere Books, 1988)

Engelberg, E., *The Vast Design: Patterns in W.B. Yeats' Aesthetic* (Toronto University Press, 1964)
Fallis, R., *The Irish Renaissance: An Introduction to Anglo-Irish Literature* (1977; repr. Gill and Macmillan, 1978)
Farag, F., *The Opposing Virtues: Two Essays, New Yeats Papers XV* (Dolmen Press, 1978)
Faulkner, P., *Yeats* (Open University Press, 1987)
Fay, G., *The Abbey Theatre: Cradle of Genius* (Hollis and Carter, 1958)
Fay, W. and Carswell, C., *The Fays of the Abbey Theatre: An Autobiographical Record* (Rich and Cowen, 1935)
Fenollosa, E. and Pound, E., *Certain Noble Plays of Japan* (Cuala Press, 1916)
Ferguson, Sir S., *Congal* (Edward Ponsonby, 1872)
Finneran, R., 'Yeats' Revisions in *The Celtic Twilight* 1912-1925', *Tulane Studies in English* 20, 1972, pp. 97- 105
— *The Prose Fiction of W.B. Yeats: The Search for 'Those Simple Forms'* (Dolmen Press, 1973)
— *Anglo-Irish Literature: A Review of Research* (The Modern Language Association of America, 1976)
— *Editing Yeats' Poems* (Macmillan, 1983)
— (ed.), *Recent Research on Anglo-Irish Writers: A Supplement to* Anglo-Irish Literature: A Review of Research (The Modern Language Association of America, 1983a)
— 'The Order of Yeats' Poems', *Irish University Review* vol. 14 no. 2 (1984), pp. 165-76
Flannery, J., 'W.B. Yeats, Gordon Craig and the Visual Arts of the Theatre' in *O'Driscoll and Reynolds (1975), pp. 82-108
— *W.B. Yeats and the Idea of a Theatre: The Early Abbey Theatre in Theory and Practice* (Yale University Press, 1976)
Flannery, M.C., *Yeats and Magic: The Earlier Works* (Gill and Macmillan, 1977)
Fletcher, I., Review of *Yeats at Songs and Choruses* in *Yeats Annual* no. 3 (Macmillan, 1985), pp. 258-63
— *W.B. Yeats and his Contemporaries* (Harvester Press, 1987)
Foster, R., *Modern Ireland 1600-1972* (Penguin, 1988)
Freyer, G., *W.B. Yeats and the Anti-Democratic Tradition* (Gill and Macmillan, 1981)
Friedman, B., *Adventures in the Deeps of the Mind: The Cuchulain Cycle of W.B. Yeats* (Princeton University Press, 1977)
Frye, N., *The Anatomy of Criticism: Four Essays* (Princeton University Press, 1957)
— *Fables of Identity: Studies in Poetic Mythology* (Harcourt Brace Jovanovich, 1963)

—— 'The Rising of the Moon: A Study of *A Vision*' in *Donoghue and Mulryne (1965), pp. 8-33
—— *Spiritus Mundi: Essays on Literature, Myth and Society* (Indiana University Press, 1976)
—— *The Secular Scripture: A Study of the Structure of Romance* (1976a; repr. Harvard University Press, 1978)
—— *The Great Code: The Bible and Literature* (Ark, 1982)
Garratt, R., *Modern Irish Poetry: Tradition and Continuity from Yeats to Heaney* (University of California Press, 1986)
Gibbon, M., *The Masterpiece and the Man: Yeats as I Knew Him* (Rupert Hart-Davis, 1959)
Gogarty, O. St John, *As I Was Going Down Sackville Street* (1937; repr. Penguin, 1954)
Goldman, A., 'Yeats, Spiritualism and Psychical Research', in *Harper (1976) pp. 108-29
Good, M., *W.B. Yeats and the Creation of a Tragic Universe* (Macmillan, 1987)
Gordon, D.J. (ed.), *W.B. Yeats: Images of a Poet* (Manchester University Press, 1961)
Gosse, E., *Father and Son: A Study of Two Temperaments* (1907; repr. Penguin, 1976)
Gould, W., 'The Editor Takes Possession', *The Times Literary Supplement*, 29 June 1984, pp. 731-3
Gregory, Lady A., *Cuchulain of Muirthemne* (1902; repr. Colin Smythe, 1976)
—— *Our Irish Theatre* (1913; repr. Capricorn, 1965)
—— *Visions and Beliefs in the West of Ireland* (1920; repr. Colin Smythe, 1970)
—— *Lady Gregory's Journals, vol. 1, Books 1-29*, ed. D. Murphy (Colin Smythe, 1978)
—— *Lady Gregory's Journals, vol. 2, Books 30-45,* ed. D. Murphy (Colin Smythe, 1987)
Grossman, A., *Poetic Knowledge in the Early Yeats: A Study of the Wind Among the Reeds* (The University Press of Virginia, 1969)
Gwynn, S. (ed.), *Scattering Branches*, reissued as *William Butler Yeats: Essays in Tribute* (1940; repr. Kennikat Press, 1965)
Hall, J. and Steinmann, M. (eds), *The Permanence of Yeats* (1950; repr. Collier Books, 1961)
Harmon, M., *Irish Poetry After Yeats* (Little, Brown and Co., 1979)
Harper, G.M., *Yeats' Golden Dawn* (Macmillan, 1974)
—— (ed.), *Yeats and the Occult* (Macmillan, 1976)
—— *W.B. Yeats and W.T. Horton: The Record of an Occult Friendship* (Humanities Press, 1980)

— *The Making of Yeats'* A Vision*: A Study of the Automatic Script*, 2 vols (Macmillan, 1987)
Harris, D., *Yeats, Coole Park and Ballylee* (Johns Hopkins, 1974)
Hassett, J., *Yeats and the Poetics of Hate* (Eire: Gill and Macmillan; USA: St Martin's Press, 1986)
Heaney, S., 'Yeats as an Example?', in *Preoccupations: Selected Prose 1968-1978* (Faber, 1980), pp. 98-114
Henn, T.R., *The Lonely Tower: Studies in the Poetry of W.B. Yeats* (Methuen, 1950)
Hill, G., ' "The Conscious Mind's Intelligible Structure": A Debate', *Agenda* vol. 9 no. 4 and vol. 10 no. 1 (Autumn/Winter 1971-2), pp. 14-23
Himber, A., *The Letters of John Quinn to William Butler Yeats* (UMI Research Press, 1983)
Hirsch, E., ' "Contention is Better Than Loneliness": The Poet as Folklorist' (1979; repr. in *Schleifer, 1980)
Hoffman, D., *Barbarous Knowledge: Myth in the Poetry of Yeats, Graves and Muir* (Oxford University Press, 1967)
Hogan, R., *After the Irish Renaissance: A Critical History of the Irish Drama Since 'The Plough and the Stars'* (Macmillan, 1968)
— and Kilroy, J., *The Irish Literary Theatre 1899-1901* (Eire: Dolmen Press; USA: Humanities Press, 1975)
— and Kilroy, J., *The Abbey Theatre: The Years of Synge 1905-1909* (Eire: Dolmen Press; USA: Humanities Press, 1978)
— and Poteet, D., *The Rise of the Realists 1910-1915* (Eire: Dolmen Press; USA: Humanities Press, 1979)
Holloway, J., *Joseph Holloway's Abbey Theatre: A Selection from his Unpublished Journal 'Impressions of a Dublin Playgoer'*, eds Hogan, R. and O' Neill, M. (Southern Illinois University Press, 1967)
Hone, J., *W.B. Yeats: 1865-1939* (Macmillan, 1942)
Hough, G., *The Last Romantics* (1947; repr. UK: Methuen; USA: Barnes and Noble, 1961)
— *The Mystery Religion of W.B. Yeats* (UK: Harvester Press; USA: Barnes and Noble, 1984)
Howarth, H., *The Irish Writers, 1880-1940: Literature Under Parnell's Star* (Rockliff, 1958)
Howe, E., *The Magicians of the Golden Dawn: A Documentary History of a Magical Order 1887-1923* (Routledge and Kegan Paul, 1972)
Hyde, D., *Beside the Fire: A Collection of Irish Gaelic Folk Stories* (Nutt, 1890)
— *Love Songs of Connacht* (Gill, 1893)

—— 'The Necessity of De-Anglicising Ireland', in Duffy, Sir C.G., *The Revival of Irish Literature* (Fisher Unwin, 1894)
Hynes, S., 'Yeats and the Poets of the Thirties', in *Modern Irish Literature: Essays in Honor of William York Tindall*, ed. Porter, R. and Brophy, J. (Twayne, 1972), pp. 1-22
Ishibashi, H., 'Yeats and the Noh: Types of Japanese Beauty and their Reflection in Yeats' Plays', in *Miller (1968), pp. 129-96
Jeffares, A.N., *W.B. Yeats: Man and Poet* (1949; rev. ed. Routledge and Kegan Paul, 1962)
—— and Cross, K. (eds), *In Excited Reverie: A Centenary Tribute To William Butler Yeats, 1865-1939* (Macmillan, 1965)
—— and Knowland, A.S., *A Commentary on the Collected Poems of W.B. Yeats* (Macmillan, 1975)
—— (ed.), *W.B. Yeats: The Critical Heritage* (Routledge and Kegan Paul, 1977)
—— *Anglo-Irish Literature* (Macmillan, 1982)
—— *A New Commentary on the Poems of W.B. Yeats* (Macmillan, 1984)
—— *W.B. Yeats: A New Biography* (Hutchinson, 1988)
Jochum, K.P.S., *W.B. Yeats: A Classified Bibliography of Criticism* (University of Illinois Press,1978)
Johnston, D., *Irish Poetry After Joyce* (USA: University of Notre Dame Press; Eire: Dolmen Press, 1985)
Jordan, C., *Terrible Beauty: The Easter Rebellion and Yeats' 'Great Tapestry'* (USA: Bucknell University Press; UK and Canada: Associated University Presses, 1987)
Kain, R., *Dublin in the Age of William Butler Yeats and James Joyce* (University of Oklahoma Press, 1962)
Kennedy, P., *Legendary Fictions of the Irish Celts* (Macmillan, 1866)
—— *The Fireside Stories of Ireland* (M'Glashan and Gill, 1870)
Kenner, H., 'The Sacred Book of the Arts' (1955; repr. in *Unterecker, 1963, pp. 10-22)
—— *A Colder Eye: The Modern Irish Writers* (1983; repr. Penguin, 1984)
—— 'The Three Deaths of Yeats', in *Yeats: An Annual of Critical and Textual Studies*, vol. v, 1987, pp. 87-94
Kermode, F., *Romantic Image* (1957; repr. Collins, 1976)
—— *The Sense of an Ending: Studies in the Theory of Fiction* (Oxford University Press, 1967)
Kinahan, F., *Yeats, Folklore and Occultism: Contexts of the Early Work and Thought* (Unwin and Hyman, 1988)
Kinsella, T., 'The Irish Writer', in *Davis, Mangan, Ferguson? Tradition and the Irish Writer* (Dolmen Press, 1970), pp. 57- 66

Kline, G., *The Last Courtly Lover: Yeats and the Idea of Woman* (UMI Research Press, 1983)
Komesu, O., *The Double Perspective of Yeats' Aesthetic* (Colin Smythe, 1984)
Kuch, P., *Yeats and AE* (Colin Smythe, 1986)
Langbaum, R., *The Mysteries of Identity: A Theme in Modern Literature* (Oxford University Press, 1977)
Leavis, F.R., *New Bearings in English Poetry: A Study of the Contemporary Situation* (1932; repr. Chatto and Windus, 1963)
—— 'Retrospect of a Decade', *Scrutiny* vol. ix (1940), repr. Leavis, F.R. (ed.) *A Selection from Scrutiny* vol. I (Cambridge University Press, 1968), pp. 175-7
Le Gallienne, R., *The Romantic '90s* (1926; repr. Putnam and Co., 1951)
Lentricchia, F., *The Gaiety of Language: An Essay on the Radical Poetics of W.B. Yeats and Wallace Stevens* (University of California Press, 1968)
Levenson, M., *A Genealogy of Modernism: A Study of English Literary Doctrine 1908-1922* (Cambridge University Press, 1984)
Levine, H., *Yeats' Daimonic Renewal* (UMI Research Press, 1983)
Lipking, L., *The Life of the Poet: Beginning and Ending Poetic Careers* (University of Chicago Press, 1981)
Litz, A.W., 'Pound and Yeats: The Road to Stone Cottage', in Bornstein, G. (ed.), *Ezra Pound Among the Poets* (University of Chicago Press, 1985), pp. 128-48
Loftus, R., *Nationalism in Modern Anglo-Irish Poetry* (University of Wisconsin Press, 1964)
Loizeaux, E.B., *Yeats and the Visual Arts* (Rutgers University Press, 1986)
Longenbach, J., *Stone Cottage: Pound, Yeats, and Modernism* (Oxford University Press, 1988)
Lucas, F.L., *The Drama of Chekhov, Synge, Yeats, and Pirandello* (Cassell, 1963)
Lucas, J., *Modern English Poetry: From Hardy to Hughes: A Critical Survey* (Batsford, 1986)
Lucy, S. (ed.), *Irish Poets in English: The Thomas Davis Lectures on Anglo-Irish Poetry* (The Mercier Press, 1973)
—— 'Metre and Movement in Anglo-Irish Verse', *Irish University Review*, vol. 8 no. 2, Autumn 1978, pp. 151-77
Lynch, D., *Yeats: The Poetics of the Self* (University of Chicago Press, 1979)
MacDonagh, T., *Literature in Ireland: Studies Irish and Anglo-Irish* (UK: Fisher Unwin; Eire: Talbot Press, 1916)

Mac Neice, L., *The Poetry of W.B. Yeats* (1941; repr. with foreword by Ellmann, R., Oxford University Press, 1969)
Malins, E., *A Preface to Yeats* (Longman, 1974)
Malone, A., *The Irish Drama 1896-1928* (Constable and Co., 1929)
Marcus, P., *Yeats and the Beginning of the Irish Renaissance* (Cornell University Press, 1970)
— 'Yeats' "Last Poems": A Reconsideration', *Yeats Annual* no. 5 (1987), pp. 3-14
Martin, G., 'The Wild Swans at Coole', in *Donoghue and Mulryne (1965), pp. 54-72
Martyn, E., 'A Plea for the Revival of the Irish Literary Theatre', *The Irish Review*, April 1914, pp. 79-84
Maxwell, D.E.S., *A Critical History of Modern Irish Drama 1891-1980* (Cambridge University Press, 1984)
— and Bushrui, S.B. (eds), *W.B. Yeats, 1865-1965: Centenary Essays on the Art of W.B. Yeats* (Nigeria: Ibadan University Press; UK: Nelson, 1965)
McCann, S. (ed.), *The Story of the Abbey Theatre* (New English Library, 1967)
McCormack, W., *Ascendancy and Tradition in Anglo-Irish Literary History from 1789 to 1939* (Clarendon Press, 1985)
McDiarmid, L., *Saving Civilisation: Yeats, Eliot and Auden Between the Wars* (Cambridge University Press, 1984)
Meir, C., *The Ballads and Songs of W.B. Yeats* (Macmillan, 1974)
Melchiori, G., *The Whole Mystery of Art: Pattern into Poetry in the Work of W.B. Yeats* (Routledge and Kegan Paul, 1960)
Mikhail, E.H., *A Bibliography of Modern Irish Drama 1899-1970* (Macmillan, 1972)
— (ed.), *W.B. Yeats, Interviews and Recollections* 2 vols (Macmillan, 1977)
Miller, J.H., *Poets of Reality: Six Twentieth-Century Writers* (USA: The Belknap Press; UK: Oxford University Press, 1966)
Miller, L. (ed.), *The Dolmen Press Yeats Centenary Papers MCMLXV* (Eire: Dolmen Press; UK: Oxford University Press; USA: Dufour Editions, 1968)
— *The Noble Drama of W.B. Yeats* (Eire: Dolmen Press; USA: Humanities Press, 1977)
Montague, J., 'What To Make of W.B. Yeats', The *Guardian*, 14 June 1984, p. 21
Moore, G., *Evelyn Innes* (T. Fisher Unwin, 1898)
— *Hail and Farewell* (1911-14; repr. ed. Cave, R., Colin Smythe, 1976)
Moore, J.R., *Masks of Love and Death: Yeats as Dramatist* (Cornell University Press, 1971)

Moore, V., *The Unicorn: William Butler Yeats' Search for Reality* (Macmillan, 1954)
Muir, E., *The Present Age From 1914* (The Cresset Press, 1939)
Murphy, F., *Yeats' Early Poetry: The Quest for Reconciliation* (Louisiana State University Press, 1975)
Murphy, W., *The Yeats Family and the Pollexfens of Sligo* (Dolmen Press, 1971)
— *Prodigal Father* (Cornell University Press, 1979)
Nathan, L., *The Tragic Drama of William Butler Yeats: Figures in a Dance* (Columbia University Press, 1965)
Neuman, S., *Some One Myth: Yeats' Autobiographical Prose* (Eire: Dolmen Press; USA: Humanities Press, 1982)
Nic Shiubhlaigh, M., *The Splendid Years* (James Duffy, 1955)
Nicoll, A., *World Drama: From Aeschylus to Anouilh* (1949; 2nd ed. Harrap, 1976)
O'Brien, C.C., 'Passion and Cunning: An Essay on the Politics of W.B. Yeats', in *Jeffares and Cross (1965), pp. 207-78
— *The Suspecting Glance* (Faber, 1972)
O'Connor, F., *A Short History of Irish Literature: A Backward Look* (UK: Macmillan; USA:Capricorn, 1967)
O'Donnell, W., 'Yeats as Adept and Artist: *The Speckled Bird*, *The Secret Rose* and *The Wind Among the Reeds*', in *Harper (1976), pp. 55-79
— *A Guide to the Prose Fiction of W.B. Yeats* (UMI Research Press, 1983)
O'Driscoll, R. and Reynolds, L. (eds), *Yeats and the Theatre* (Macmillan, 1975)
O'Grady, S.J., *History of Ireland: The Heroic Period* (Eire: Ponsonby; UK: Sampson Low, 1878)
— *History of Ireland: Critical and Philosophical* vol. I (Eire: Ponsonby; UK: Sampson Low, 1881)
— *The Crisis in Ireland* (Eire: Ponsonby; UK: Simpkin and Marshall, 1882)
— *Toryism and Tory Democracy* (Chapman and Hall, 1886)
— *The Coming of Cuculain* (1894; repr. Eire: Talbot Press; UK: T. Fisher Unwin, 1920)
— *The Story of Ireland* (Methuen, 1894a)
— *All Ireland* (Eire: Sealy, Bryers and Walker; UK: T. Fisher Unwin, 1898)
— 'The Great Enchantment', *All Ireland Review*, vol. I no. 4, 27 January 1900, p. 1
O hAodha, M., *Theatre in Ireland* (Basil Blackwell, 1974)
O'Hanlon, J., *Irish Folk Lore: Traditions and Superstitions of the Country; with Humorous Tales* (Cameron and Ferguson, 1870)

O'Hara, D., *Tragic Knowledge: Yeats' Autobiography and Hermeneutics* (Columbia University Press, 1981)
Olney, J., *The Rhizome and the Flower: The Perennial Philosophy – Yeats and Jung* (University of California Press, 1980)
—— (ed.), *Autobiography: Essays Theoretical and Critical* (Princeton University Press, 1980a)
Orwell, G., 'Inside the Whale' (1940), repr. in *Inside the Whale and Other Essays* (Penguin, 1972), pp. 9-50
O'Shea, E., *A Descriptive Catalog of W.B. Yeats' Library* (Garland Publishing Inc., 1985)
Parkin, A., *The Dramatic Imagination of W.B. Yeats* (Eire: Gill and Macmillan; USA: Barnes and Noble, 1978)
Parkinson, T., *W.B. Yeats Self-Critic: A Study of his Early Verse* (1951), repr. in *W.B. Yeats Self-Critic and W.B. Yeats: The Later Poetry* (University of California Press, 1971)
—— *W.B. Yeats: The Later Poetry* (1964), repr. in *W.B. Yeats Self-Critic and W.B. Yeats: The Later Poetry* (University of California Press, 1971)
Parrish, S. and Painter, J. (eds), *A Concordance to the Poems of W.B. Yeats* (Cornell University Press, 1963)
Peacock, R., *The Poet in the Theatre* (1946; repr. MacGibbon and Kee, 1961)
Perloff, M.,' "The Tradition of Myself": The Autobiographical Mode of W.B. Yeats', *Journal of Modern Literature* 4 (1975), pp. 529-73
Peterson, R., *William Butler Yeats* (Twayne Publishers, 1982)
Pollock, J.H., *William Butler Yeats* (UK: Gerald Duckworth and Co.; Eire: Talbot Press, 1935)
Power, P., *The Story of Anglo-Irish Poetry 1800-1922* (Mercier Press, 1967)
Pritchard, W. (ed.), *W.B. Yeats: A Critical Anthology* (Penguin, 1972)
Putzel, S., *Reconstructing Yeats: The Secret Rose and The Wind Among the Reeds* (Gill and Macmillan, 1986)
Rajan, B., *W.B. Yeats: A Critical Introduction* (Hutchinson, 1965)
Raine, K., *Yeats the Initiate: Essays on Certain Themes in the Work of W.B. Yeats* (Eire: Dolmen Press; UK: George Allen and Unwin, 1986)
Reid, B., *The Man from New York: John Quinn and His Friends* (Oxford University Press, 1968)
Ricks, C., 'Trick of the Voice', *The Sunday Times*, 20 May 1984, p. 43
Robinson, L., *Curtain Up: An Autobiography* (Michael Joseph, 1942)

— *Ireland's Abbey Theatre: A History 1899-1951* (Sidgwick and Jackson, 1951)
Ronsley, J., *Yeats' Autobiography: Life as Symbolic Pattern* (USA: Harvard University Press; UK: Oxford University Press, 1968)
— 'Yeats as an Autobiographical Poet', in Ronsley, J. (ed.), *Myth and Reality in Irish Literature* (Wilfrid Laurier University Press, 1977), pp. 131-48
Rosenthal, M., *The Modern Poets: A Critical Introduction* (1960; repr. Oxford University Press, 1965)
Rudd, M., *Divided Image: A Study of William Blake and W.B. Yeats* (Routledge and Kegan Paul, 1953)
Russell, G. (AE), *The Interpreters* (Macmillan, 1922)
Said, E., *Nationalism, Colonialism and Literature: Yeats and Decolonization* (Field Day Theatre Company, 1988)
Saul, G.B., *Prolegomena to the Study of Yeats' Poems* (Oxford University Press, 1957)
— *Prolegomena to the Study of Yeats' Plays* (Oxford University Press, 1958)
Schleifer, R. (ed.), *The Genres of the Irish Literary Revival* (USA: Pilgrim Books; Eire: Wolfhound, 1980)
Schriker, G., *A New Species of Man: The Poetic Persona of W.B. Yeats* (USA: Bucknell University Press, 1982)
Schwartz, S., *The Matrix of Modernism: Pound, Eliot and Early Twentieth-Century Thought* (Princeton University Press, 1986)
Seward, B., *The Symbolic Rose* (Columbia University Press, 1960)
Sidnell, M., 'Unacceptable Hypotheses: The New Edition of Yeats' Poems and Its Making', *Yeats Annual* no. 3 (1985), pp. 225-43
Siegmund-Schultze, D. (ed.), *Irland: Gesellschaft Und Kultur* (Martin-Luther-Universität, 1987)
Sisson, C.H., *English Poetry 1900-1950: An Assessment* (Carcanet New Press, 1981)
Skelton, R. and Saddlemyer, A. (eds), *The World of W.B. Yeats* (1965; rev. ed. University of Washington Press, 1967)
Skene, R., *The Cuchulain Plays of W.B. Yeats* (Macmillan, 1974)
Snukal, R., *High Talk: The Philosophical Poetry of W.B. Yeats* (Cambridge University Press, 1973)
The Southern Review: William Butler Yeats Memorial Issue, VII 3 (winter 1941-2)
Spears, M.K., *Dionysus and the City: Modernism in Twentieth-Century Poetry* (Oxford University Press, 1970)
Spender, S., *The Destructive Element: A Study of Modern Writers and Beliefs* (Jonathan Cape, 1935)
Stallworthy, J., *Between the Lines: Yeats' Poetry in the Making* (1963; repr. Clarendon Press, 1965)

— (ed.), *Yeats: Last Poems: A Casebook* (Macmillan, 1968)

— *Vision and Revision in Yeats' 'Last Poems'* (Clarendon Press, 1969)

Stanfield, P.S., *Yeats and Politics in the 1930s* (Macmillan, 1988)

Stauffer, D., *The Golden Nightingale: Essays on Some Principles of Poetry in the Lyrics of William Butler Yeats* (Macmillan, 1949)

Stead, C.K., *The New Poetic: Yeats to Eliot* (1964; repr. Penguin, 1967)

— *Pound, Yeats, Eliot and the Modernist Movement* (Macmillan, 1986)

Stock, A.G., *W.B. Yeats: His Poetry and Thought* (1961; repr. Cambridge University Press, 1964)

Symons, A., *The Symbolist Movement in Literature* (1899; repr. E.P. Dutton, 1958)

Tate, A., 'Yeats' Romanticism: Notes and Suggestions', *The Southern Review* 1942, pp. 591-600

Taylor, R., 'Assimilation and Accomplishment: No Drama and an Unpublished Source for *At the Hawk's Well*', in *O'Driscoll and Reynolds (1975), pp. 137-58

— *The Drama of W.B. Yeats: Irish Myth and the Japanese No* (Yale University Press, 1976)

— *A Reader's Guide to the Plays of W.B. Yeats* (Macmillan, 1984)

Thatcher, D., *Nietzsche in England 1890-1914: The Growth of a Reputation* (University of Toronto Press, 1970)

Thompson, W.I., *The Imagination of an Insurrection: Dublin, Easter 1916: A Study of an Ideological Movement* (1967; repr. The Lindisfarne Press, 1982)

Thuente, M.H., *Yeats and Irish Folklore* (Barnes and Noble, 1981)

Thurley, G., *The Turbulent Dream: Passion and Politics in the Poetry of W.B. Yeats* (Queensland University Press, 1983)

Tindall, W.Y., 'The Symbolism of W.B. Yeats', (1945); repr. in *Unterecker (1963), pp. 43-53

Torchiana, D., *Yeats and Georgian Ireland* (Northwestern University Press, 1966)

Tuohy, F., *Yeats* (Macmillan, 1976)

Unterecker, J., *A Reader's Guide to W.B. Yeats* (1959; repr. Thames and Hudson, 1975)

— (ed.), *Yeats: A Collection of Critical Essays* (Prentice Hall, 1963)

Ure, P., *W.B. Yeats* (Oliver and Boyd, 1963)

— *Yeats the Playwright: A Commentary on Character and Design in the Major Plays* (Routledge and Kegan Paul, 1963a)

— *Yeats and Anglo-Irish Literature: Critical Essays by Peter Ure* (Liverpool University Press, 1974)

Vendler, H., *Yeats' Vision and the Later Plays* (Harvard University Press, 1963)
Wade, A., *A Bibliography of the Writings of W.B. Yeats*, 3rd ed., rev. Alspach, R.K. (Rupert Hart-Davis, 1968)
Waley, A., *The No Plays of Japan* (1920; repr. Grove Press, 1957)
Watson, G., *Irish Identity and the Literary Revival: Synge, Yeats, Joyce and O'Casey* (Croom Helm, 1979)
Webster, B., *Yeats: A Psychoanalytic Study* (Macmillan, 1974)
Welch, R., *Irish Poetry From Moore to Yeats* (Colin Smythe, 1980)
Whitaker, T., *Swan and Shadow: Yeats' Dialogue with History* (University of North Carolina Press, 1964)
Wilson, E., *Axel's Castle: A Study in the Imaginative Literature of 1870-1930* (1931; repr. Collins, 1967)
Wilson, F.A.C., *Yeats and Tradition* (1958; repr. Methuen, 1968)
—— *Yeats' Iconography* (1960; repr. Methuen, 1969)
Winters, Y., *The Poetry of W.B. Yeats* (Alan Swallow, 1960)
Worth, K., *The Irish Drama of Europe from Yeats to Beckett* (The Athlone Press, 1978)
Wright, D., *Yeats' Myth of the Self: The Autobiographical Prose* (Eire: Gill and Macmillan; USA: Barnes and Noble, 1987)
Yeats, J.B., *Early Memories: Some Chapters of Autobiography* (Cuala Press, 1923)
—— *J.B. Yeats: Letters to his Son, W.B. Yeats, and Others, 1869-1922*, ed. Hone, J. (Faber, 1944)
Yeats, M., 'W.B. Yeats and the Irish Folk Song', *Southern Folklore Quarterly*, vol. 31 no. 2 (June 1966), pp. 153-78
Yeats Annual, ed. Gould, W. (Macmillan, 1982-)
Yeats: An Annual of Critical and Textual Studies, ed. Finneran, R. (UMI Research Press, 1983-)
Young, D., *Troubled Mirror: A Study of Yeats'* The Tower (Iowa University Press, 1987)
Young, Dudley, *Out of Ireland: A Reading of Yeats' Poetry* (Carcanet Press, 1975)
Zwerdling, A., *Yeats and the Heroic Ideal* (New York University Press, 1965)